Aluna Publishing House is united by our shared passion for education, languages, and technology. Our mission is to provide the ultimate learning experience when it comes to books. We believe that books are not just words on paper; they are gateways to knowledge, imagination, and enlightenment.

Through our collective expertise, we aim to bridge the gap between traditional learning and the digital age, harnessing the power of technology to make books more accessible, interactive, and enjoyable. We are dedicated to creating a platform that fosters a love for reading, language, and lifelong learning. Join us on our journey as we embark on a quest to redefine the way you experience books.

Let's unlock the limitless potential of knowledge, one page at a time.

TABLE OF CONTENTS

Introduction……………………………………………………**13**

What is an Algorithm?…………………………………….**14**

Data Structures……………………………………………..**15**

  Array……………………………………………………………**16**

    Equilibrium Index in Array………………………………17

    Find Triplets with 0 Sum…………………………………18

    Index 2d Array in 1d………………………………………19

    Kth Largest Element………………………………………20

    Median Two Array…………………………………………21

    Monotonic Array……………………………………………22

    Pairs with Given Sum……………………………………..23

    Permutations…………………………………………………24

    Prefix Sum……………………………………………………25

    Product Sum…………………………………………………26

    Sparse Table…………………………………………………27

  Binary Tree………………………………………………….**28**

    AVL Tree………………………………………………………29

    Binary Search Recursive…………………………………31

    Binary Tree Mirror…………………………………………32

    Binary Node Sum……………………………………………33

    Binary Path Sum……………………………………………34

    Binary Tree Traversals……………………………………35

    Diameter of Binary Tree…………………………………36

    Diff Views of Binary Tree……………………………….38

    Distribute Coins……………………………………………40

    Fenwick Tree…………………………………………………41

    Floor and Ceiling……………………………………………...42

    Is Sorted…………………………………………………………..43

    Is Sum Tree……………………………………………………...44

    Lowest Common Ancestor……………………………………...46

    Maximum Fenwick Tree………………………………………...47

    Number of Possible Binary Trees…………………………48

Disjoint Set………………………………………………………..49

Hashing……………………………………………………………51

    Bloom Filter……………………………………………………….52

    Double Hash……………………………………………………...54

    Hash Map………………………………………………………….56

    Hash Table………………………………………………………...58

    Hash Table with Linked List…………………………….60

    Quadratic Probing………………………………………………63

Heap………………………………………………………………….65

    Binomial Heap…………………………………………………...67

    Heap Generic…………………………………………………….70

    Max Heap………………………………………………………….72

    Min Heap…………………………………………………………..74

    Randomized Heap……………………………………………….76

    Skew Heap………………………………………………………...78

Kdtree………………………………………………………………80

    Build Kdtree……………………………………………………...81

    Hypercube Points……………………………………………….83

    Kd Node……………………………………………………………84

    Nearest Neighbour Search……………………………………...85

Linked List………………………………………………………..86

    Floyds Cycle Detection………………………………………….87

    From Sequence…………………………………………………...88

Has Loop……………………………………………………..89

Middle Element of Linked List……………………….90

Print Reverse……………………………………………….91

Swap Nodes…………………………………………………92

Queue……………………………………………………………93

Priority Queue Using List………………………………..94

Queue by List……………………………………………....95

Stacks……………………………………………………………...96

Balanced Parenthesis…………………………………..97

Infix to Postfix Conversion……………………………..98

Next Greater Element………………………………….99

Postfix Evaluation………………………………………..100

Prefix Evaluation…………………………………………..101

Stock Span Problem…………………………………….102

Sorting Algorithms………………………………………….103

Bogo Sort…………………………………………………..104

Bubble Sort………………………………………………...105

Counting Sort……………………………………………...106

Double Sort (Hybrid Sort Approach)…………………...107

Dutch National Flag Sort………………………………108

Exchange Sort…………………………………………....109

Gnome Sort………………………………………………...110

Insertion Sort……………………………………………...111

Msd Radix Sort……………………………………………112

Natural Sort………………………………………………...113

Odd Even Sort…………………………………………….114

Quick Sort…………………………………………………..115

Selection Sort……………………………………………..116

Shell Sort…………………………………………………...117

6

 Shrink Shell Sort………………………………………..118

 SlowSort……………………………………………….119

 Stooge Sort……………………………………………120

 Unknown Sort………………………………………...122

 Wiggle Sort…………………………………………...123

Searching Algorithms……………………………………124

 Binary Search……………………………………….**125**
 Double Linear Search……………………………...**126**
 Hill Climbing………………………………………..**127**
 Interpolation Search………………………………**129**
 Jump Search………………………………………..**130**
 Linear Search………………………………………**131**
 Median of Medians…………………………………**132**
 Quick Select………………………………………..**134**
 Simulated Annealing……………………………….**137**
 Tabu Search………………………………………..**139**
 Ternary Search……………………………………..**142**

Dynamic Programming………………………………….144

 Catalan Numbers…………………………………..**145**
 Climbing Stairs…………………………………….**146**
 Combination Sum Lv………………………………**147**
 Edit Distance……………………………………….**148**
 Factorial…………………………………………….**149**
 Fast Fibonacci……………………………………..**150**
 Fizz Buzz……………………………………………**151**
 Integer Partition…………………………………..**152**
 Longest Common Substring……………………..**153**
 Palindrome Partitioning…………………………..**154**
 Tribonacci………………………………………….**155**
 Word Break………………………………………...**156**
 Coin Change………………………………………..**157**

Ciphers..**158**
   Affine Cipher..**159**
   Atbash..**161**
   Base 16..**162**
   Beaufor Cipher...**164**
   Caesar Cipher...**166**
   Morse Code...**168**
   Rot 13..**170**
   Rsa Cipher..**171**
   Rsa Key Generator...**173**
   Suffled Shift Cipher..**175**
Maths..**177**
     Abs
     ....
    178
     Addition without Arithmetic................................179
     Aliquot Sum...181
     Arc Length..182
     Average Absolute Deviation................................183
     Average Mean...184
     Average Median..185
     Average Mode...186
     Bailey Borwein Plouffe...187
     Base Neg 2 Conversion.......................................188
     Binary Exponentiation..189
     Binary Multiplication..190
     Binomial Coefficient...191
     Binomial Distribution...193
     Ceil
     ....
      195

Chebyshev Distance…………………………………………..196
Check Polygon…………………………………………………..197
Chudnovsky Algorithm………………………………………198
Collatz Sequence………………………………………………199
Combinations…………………………………………………...200
Continued Fraction…………………………………………...201
Decimal Isolate………………………………………………….202
Decimal to Fraction…………………………………………….203
Double Factorial………………………………………………..204
Entropy……………………………………………………………..205
Euclidean Distance……………………………………………..206
Extended Euclidean Algorithm…………………………….207
Factors……………………………………………………………...208
Find Max……………………………………………………………209
Floor…………………………………………………………………212
Gamma……………………………………………………………..214

Digital Image Processing……………………………………………215

Change Brightness……………………………………………...216
Change Contrast………………………………………………..218
Convert to Negative…………………………………………….219
Burkes……………………………………………………………….220
Canny………………………………………………………………..222
Bilateral Filter…………………………………………………….223
Convolve…………………………………………………………...224
Gabor Filter……………………………………………………….225
Gaussian Filter……………………………………………………227
Laplacian Filter…………………………………………………..228
Local Binary Pattern……………………………………………229
Median Filter……………………………………………………..231

Sobel Filter……………………………………………………233

Histogram Stretch……………………………………………235

Index Calculation……………………………………………237

Dilation Operation……………………………………………240

Erosion Operation……………………………………………241

Resize…………………………………………………………242

Rotation………………………………………………………243

Sepia…………………………………………………………245

Strings………………………………………………………247

Alternative String Arrange…………………………………248

Anagram………………………………………………………253

Barcode Validator……………………………………………256

Bitap String Match……………………………………………257

Camel Case to Snake Case…………………………………258

Capitalize……………………………………………………259

Check Anagram………………………………………………260

Count Vowels…………………………………………………261

Credit Card Validator…………………………………………262

Detecting English Programmatically………………………263

Is Srilankan Phone Number…………………………………264

Is Valid Email Address………………………………………265

Join
  ……………………………………………………………
  ……………………………………………………………266

Levenshtein Distance………………………………………268

Lower…………………………………………………………270

Naive String Search…………………………………………271

Ngram…………………………………………………………272

Pig Latin………………………………………………………273

Prefix Function………………………………………………274

10

Remove Duplicate…………………………………………..275
Reverse Letters………………………………………….278
Reverse Words…………………………………………280
Split……………………………………………………282
Top K Frequent Words…………………………………..284
Wave String……………………………………………285
Word Patterns…………………………………………..286
Z Function……………………………………………..287

Machine Learning……………………………………..288

Automatic Differentiation……………………………291
Data Transformations…………………………………293
Decision Tree…………………………………………294
Dimensionality Reduction……………………………..296
Frequent Pattern Growth………………………………297
K Means Clust………………………………………..298
Linear Regression……………………………………..300
Local Wighted Learning………………………………302
Logistic Regression…………………………………..304
Loss Functions………………………………………..306
Lstm Prediction………………………………………307

Neural Network………………………………………..308

Activation Functions…………………………………..309
Binary Step…………………………………………….310
Exponential Linear Unit………………………………..311
Gaussian Error Unit…………………………………….312
Leaky Rectified Linear unit……………………………..313
mish……………………………………………………314
squareplus……………………………………………..315
Convultion Neural Network……………………………316
Simple Neural Network………………………………..318

11

- Two Hidden Layers……………………………………...320
- Graphs……………………………………………………….322
  - A Star…………………………………………………….323
  - Ant Colony Optimization……………………………….325
  - Breadth First Search……………………………………328
  - Check Bipatrite…………………………………………..329
  - Check Cycle……………………………………………...330
  - Connected Components………………………………..331
  - Finding Fridges………………………………………….332

Introduction

This book provides an essential collection of algorithms designed to help you solve a wide range of programming problems. It's perfect for beginners looking to gain key knowledge and improve their skills efficiently.

With clear and practical explanations, this book serves as an excellent guide for those just starting their programming journey, offering a solid foundation to help them progress quickly.

What is an Algorithm?

An algorithm is essentially a sequence of instructions designed to process one or more inputs, carry out specific computations or manipulations, and then deliver an output or a set of outputs. In essence, algorithms simplify tasks. Whether handling intricate data operations or executing basic calculations, they consistently follow a series of steps to yield a valuable outcome. For instance, consider a basic algorithm: a function that accepts two numbers, computes their sum, and outputs the result.

Data Structures

Data structures are specialized formats for organizing, storing, and managing data in a way that enables efficient access and modification. They provide a framework for handling data so that operations like searching, inserting, deleting, or modifying data can be performed effectively. Choosing the right data structure can significantly affect the performance of an algorithm or a program.

Here are some common types of data structures:

- **Arrays**: A collection of elements, each identified by an index or key, where all elements are stored contiguously in memory.
- **Linked Lists**: A sequence of elements, where each element points to the next one, allowing for efficient insertions and deletions at any point.
- **Stacks**: A collection of elements that follows the Last In, First Out (LIFO) principle, where only the top element can be accessed or modified.
- **Queues**: A collection of elements that follows the First In, First Out (FIFO) principle, where elements are added at the rear and removed from the front.
- **Trees**: A hierarchical structure where each element (node) has a parent and possibly several children, often used to represent hierarchical relationships.
- **Graphs**: A collection of nodes (vertices) connected by edges, used to model relationships between objects, such as networks.
- **Hash Tables**: A data structure that maps keys to values using a hash function, allowing for fast lookups, insertions, and deletions.

Each data structure is suited to specific kinds of tasks, and choosing the right one depends on the nature of the problem you're solving.

Array

An array is a data structure consisting of a collection of elements, of same memory size, each identified by at least one array index or key. An array is stored such that the position of each element can be computed from its index tuple by a mathematical formula.

Equilibrium Index in Array

The equilibrium index in an array is a position where the sum of elements on the left is equal to the sum of elements on the right. It is useful in various algorithms, particularly in finding balance points in data. The goal is to identify such an index efficiently using a linear time complexity approach.

```python
def find_equilibrium_index(arr):
    total_sum = sum(arr)
    left_sum = 0

    for i, num in enumerate(arr):
        right_sum = total_sum - left_sum - num

        if left_sum == right_sum:
            return i

        left_sum += num

    return -1  # No equilibrium index found

# Example usage:
arr = [-7, 1, 5, 2, -4, 3, 0]
index = find_equilibrium_index(arr)
print(f'Equilibrium Index: {index}')
# Output: Equilibrium Index: 3
```

Find Triplets with 0 Sum

The problem is to find all unique triplets in an array that sum to zero. Given an array of integers, the task is to find triplets (three numbers) whose sum is zero. These triplets should be distinct, meaning the same combination of numbers should not appear more than once.

```python
def find_triplets_with_zero_sum(arr):
    arr.sort()
    triplets = []

    for i in range(len(arr) - 2):
        if i > 0 and arr[i] == arr[i - 1]:
            continue
        left, right = i + 1, len(arr) - 1
        while left < right:
            s = arr[i] + arr[left] + arr[right]
            if s == 0:
                triplets.append([arr[i], arr[left], arr[right]])
                left += 1
                right -= 1
                while left < right and arr[left] == arr[left - 1]: left += 1
                while left < right and arr[right] == arr[right + 1]: right -= 1
            elif s < 0: left += 1
            else: right -= 1

    return triplets

# Example usage:
arr = [-1, 0, 1, 2, -1, -4]
print(find_triplets_with_zero_sum(arr))
# Output: [[-1, -1, 2], [-1, 0, 1]]
```

Index 2d Array in 1d

To access elements of a 2D array using a 1D array index, you can convert the 2D array into a 1D array by flattening it. The goal is to find the 1D index corresponding to any (row, column) of a 2D array. For an array with m rows and n columns, the index for an element at position (i, j) can be computed as:

$$\text{index} = i \times n + j$$

Where i is the row number, and j is the column number.

```python
def index_2d_to_1d(row, col, num_cols):
    return row * num_cols + col


# Example usage:
row, col, num_cols = 2, 3, 4
index = index_2d_to_1d(row, col, num_cols)
print(f'1D index: {index}')  # Output: 1D index: 11
```

For a 2D array with 4 columns, the element at position (2, 3) corresponds to index 11 in a flattened 1D array.

Example:

2D array:

```
[
  [0, 1,  2,  3],
  [4, 5,  6,  7],
  [8, 9, 10, 11]
]
```

Flattened 1D array:

`[0, 1, 2, 3, 4, 5, 6, 7, 8, 9, 10, 11]`

Element at (2, 3) = 11, which is at index 11 in the 1D array.

Kth Largest Element

The task is to find the Kth largest element in an unsorted array. The Kth largest element means the element that would be at position K if the array were sorted in descending order. There are several approaches to solve this, such as sorting the array or using a min-heap.

```python
def kth_largest(arr, k):
    return sorted(arr, reverse=True)[k-1]

# Example usage:
arr = [3, 2, 1, 5, 6, 4]
k = 2
print(kth_largest(arr, k))   # Output: 5
```

Median Two Array

The task is to find the median of two sorted arrays. The median is the middle element in a sorted list of numbers. If the total number of elements is even, the median is the average of the two middle elements. The challenge is to solve this problem efficiently in $O(\log(\min(m,n)))$ time complexity.

```python
def find_median_sorted_arrays(nums1, nums2):
    merged = sorted(nums1 + nums2)
    n = len(merged)

    if n % 2 == 1:
        return merged[n // 2]
    else:
        return (merged[n // 2 - 1] + merged[n // 2]) / 2

# Example usage:
nums1 = [1, 3]
nums2 = [2]
print(find_median_sorted_arrays(nums1, nums2))
# Output: 2.0
```

Monotonic Array

An array is said to be **monotonic** if it is either entirely non-increasing or non-decreasing. Your task is to determine whether a given array is monotonic. That means the array is either sorted in increasing order or decreasing order, or all the elements are equal.

```python
def is_monotonic(arr):
    increasing = decreasing = True

    for i in range(1, len(arr)):
        if arr[i] > arr[i - 1]:
            decreasing = False
        if arr[i] < arr[i - 1]:
            increasing = False

    return increasing or decreasing

# Example usage:
arr = [1, 2, 2, 3]
print(is_monotonic(arr))    # Output: True

arr = [6, 5, 4, 4]
print(is_monotonic(arr))    # Output: True

arr = [1, 3, 2]
print(is_monotonic(arr))    # Output: False
```

Pairs with Given Sum

The task is to find all pairs of elements in an array that sum up to a given target. Each pair should only be listed once. The challenge can be solved using different approaches, such as using a hash set to store the required values for the sum or sorting the array and using the two-pointer technique.

```python
def find_pairs_with_sum(arr, target):
    seen = set()
    pairs = []

    for num in arr:
        diff = target - num
        if diff in seen:
            pairs.append((diff, num))
        seen.add(num)

    return pairs

# Example usage:
arr = [1, 5, 7, -1, 5]
target = 6
print(find_pairs_with_sum(arr, target))
# Output: [(1, 5), (7, -1), (1, 5)]
```

Permutations

The task is to generate all possible permutations of a given array. A permutation is an arrangement of all the elements in a specific order. The challenge is often approached using recursion or iterative methods to ensure all combinations are explored.

```python
def permute(nums):
    def backtrack(start):
        if start == len(nums):
            permutations.append(nums[:])  # Add a copy of the current permutation
            return

        for i in range(start, len(nums)):
            nums[start], nums[i] = nums[i], nums[start]  # Swap
            backtrack(start + 1)
            nums[start], nums[i] = nums[i], nums[start]  # Backtrack (swap back)

    permutations = []
    backtrack(0)
    return permutations

# Example usage:
arr = [1, 2, 3]
print(permute(arr))
# Output: [[1, 2, 3], [1, 3, 2], [2, 1, 3], [2, 3, 1], [3, 1, 2], [3, 2, 1]]
```

Prefix Sum

The prefix sum array is a derived array that allows you to quickly calculate the sum of elements in a specific range of the original array. The prefix sum at index `i` represents the sum of all elements from the start of the array up to index `i`. This is useful for efficiently querying the sum of subarrays.

```python
def prefix_sum(arr):
    prefix = [0] * (len(arr) + 1)

    for i in range(len(arr)):
        prefix[i + 1] = prefix[i] + arr[i]

    return prefix

# Example usage:
arr = [1, 2, 3, 4, 5]
prefix = prefix_sum(arr)
print(prefix)  # Output: [0, 1, 3, 6, 10, 15]
```

Product Sum

The product sum of an array is a variation of the sum where you multiply each element of the array by its depth level. If the element is an integer, its contribution to the product sum is simply the integer multiplied by its depth. If the element is an array, you recursively calculate its product sum by increasing the depth.

```python
def product_sum(arr, depth=1):
    total = 0

    for elem in arr:
        if isinstance(elem, list):
            total += product_sum(elem, depth + 1)  # Recurse for nested arrays
        else:
            total += elem

    return total * depth

# Example usage:
arr = [1, 2, [3, 4, [5]], 5]
result = product_sum(arr)
print(result)   # Output: 43
```

Sparse Table

A Sparse Table is a data structure that enables efficient querying of the minimum or maximum in a static array over a range of indices. It preprocesses the data in O(n log n) time, allowing queries to be answered in O(1) time.

```python
import math

class SparseTable:
    def __init__(self, arr):
        self.n = len(arr)
        self.log = math.ceil(math.log2(self.n)) + 1
        self.table = [[0] * self.log for _ in range(self.n)]

        # Initialize the first column of the table
        for i in range(self.n):
            self.table[i][0] = arr[i]

        # Build the Sparse Table
        for j in range(1, self.log):
            for i in range(self.n - (1 << j) + 1):
                self.table[i][j] = min(self.table[i][j - 1], self.table[i + (1 << (j - 1))][j - 1])

    def range_min_query(self, left, right):
        j = int(math.log2(right - left + 1))
        return min(self.table[left][j], self.table[right - (1 << j) + 1][j])

# Example usage:
arr = [1, 3, 2, 7, 9, 11]
sparse_table = SparseTable(arr)

# Range minimum query from index 1 to 4
result = sparse_table.range_min_query(1, 4)
print(result)  # Output: 2
```

Binary Tree

A Binary Tree is a hierarchical data structure in which each node has at most two children, referred to as the left and right children. Binary trees are fundamental in computer science for various applications, including search trees, heaps, and expression parsing.

AVL Tree

An AVL Tree is a self-balancing binary search tree where the difference in heights between the left and right subtrees (the balance factor) is at most one for all nodes. This balancing ensures that the tree remains approximately balanced, leading to O(log n) time complexity for insertions, deletions, and lookups.

```python
class TreeNode:
    def __init__(self, value):
        self.value, self.left, self.right, self.height = value, None, None, 1

class AVLTree:
    def insert(self, root, value):
        if not root:
            return TreeNode(value)
        if value < root.value:
            root.left = self.insert(root.left, value)
        else:
            root.right = self.insert(root.right, value)

        root.height = 1 + max(self.get_height(root.left), self.get_height(root.right))
        return self.balance(root)

    def balance(self, node):
        if (b := self.get_balance(node)) > 1:
            return self.rotate_right(node) if self.get_balance(node.left) >= 0 else self.rotate_right(node.left)
        if b < -1:
            return self.rotate_left(node) if self.get_balance(node.right) <= 0 else self.rotate_left(node.right)
        return node

    def rotate_left(self, z):
        y = z.right
        z.right, y.left = y.left, z
```

```python
        z.height = 1 + max(self.get_height(z.left), self.get_height(z.right))
        y.height = 1 + max(self.get_height(y.left), self.get_height(y.right))
        return y

    def rotate_right(self, z):
        y = z.left
        z.left, y.right = y.right, z
        z.height = 1 + max(self.get_height(z.left), self.get_height(z.right))
        y.height = 1 + max(self.get_height(y.left), self.get_height(y.right))
        return y

    def get_height(self, node):
        return node.height if node else 0

    def get_balance(self, node):
        return self.get_height(node.left) - self.get_height(node.right)

    def inorder_traversal(self, node):
        return self.inorder_traversal(node.left) + [node.value] + self.inorder_traversal(node.right) if node else []

# Example usage:
avl_tree, root = AVLTree(), None
for value in [10, 20, 30, 40, 50, 25]:
    root = avl_tree.insert(root, value)

print(avl_tree.inorder_traversal(root))
# Output: [10, 20, 25, 30, 40, 50]
```

Binary Search Recursive

Recursive Binary Search is a method to efficiently find an element in a sorted array. By repeatedly dividing the search interval in half, it reduces the time complexity to O(log n). If the value is found, its index is returned; otherwise, the search continues until the element is not found.

```python
def binary_search(arr, target, left, right):
    if left > right:
        return -1  # Target not found
    mid = left + (right - left) // 2
    if arr[mid] == target:
        return mid  # Target found
    return binary_search(arr, target, left, mid - 1) if target < arr[mid] else binary_search(arr, target, mid + 1, right)

# Example usage:
arr = [1, 2, 3, 4, 5, 6, 7, 8, 9, 10]
target = 7
result = binary_search(arr, target, 0, len(arr) - 1)
print(result)  # Output: 6 (index of target)
```

Binary Tree Mirror

A binary tree mirror transformation creates a mirror image of the tree. This involves swapping the left and right children of each node recursively, resulting in a tree that reflects the original structure across its vertical axis.

```python
class TreeNode:
    def __init__(self, value):
        self.value, self.left, self.right = value, None, None

class BinaryTree:
    def mirror(self, node):
        if node:
            node.left, node.right = node.right, node.left  # Swap children
            self.mirror(node.left)   # Mirror left subtree
            self.mirror(node.right)  # Mirror right subtree

    def inorder_traversal(self, node):
        return self.inorder_traversal(node.left) + [node.value] + self.inorder_traversal(node.right) if node else []

# Example usage:
root = TreeNode(1)
root.left, root.right = TreeNode(2), TreeNode(3)
root.left.left, root.left.right = TreeNode(4), TreeNode(5)

tree = BinaryTree()
print("Inorder before mirroring:", tree.inorder_traversal(root))
# Output: [4, 2, 5, 1, 3]

tree.mirror(root)
print("Inorder after mirroring:", tree.inorder_traversal(root))
# Output: [3, 1, 5, 2, 4]
```

Binary Node Sum

The Binary Tree Node Sum operation calculates the sum of all the node values in a binary tree. This can be done using a recursive approach, where the sum of each node is obtained by adding its value to the sums of its left and right subtrees.

```python
class TreeNode:
    def __init__(self, value):
        self.value, self.left, self.right = value, None, None

class BinaryTree:
    def sum_nodes(self, node):
        if not node:
            return 0  # Base case: return 0 if the node is None
        return node.value + self.sum_nodes(node.left) + self.sum_nodes(node.right)  # Recursive sum

# Example usage:
root = TreeNode(1)
root.left, root.right = TreeNode(2), TreeNode(3)
root.left.left, root.left.right = TreeNode(4), TreeNode(5)

tree = BinaryTree()
total_sum = tree.sum_nodes(root)
print(total_sum)  # Output: 15 (1 + 2 + 3 + 4 + 5)
```

Binary Path Sum

The Binary Tree Path Sum operation checks if there exists a path from the root to any leaf node such that the sum of the values along the path equals a specified target sum. This can be achieved through a depth-first search (DFS) approach, recursively subtracting the node values from the target as you traverse down the tree.

```
class TreeNode:
    def __init__(self, value):
        self.value, self.left, self.right = value, None, None

class BinaryTree:
    def has_path_sum(self, node, target):
        if not node:
            return target == 0  # Base case: check if target is achieved
        target -= node.value  # Subtract the current node's value
        # Check both left and right subtrees
        return self.has_path_sum(node.left, target) or self.has_path_sum(node.right, target)

# Example usage:
root = TreeNode(5)
root.left, root.right = TreeNode(4), TreeNode(8)
root.left.left, root.left.right = TreeNode(11), TreeNode(2)
root.right.left, root.right.right = TreeNode(13), TreeNode(4)

tree = BinaryTree()
target_sum = 22
result = tree.has_path_sum(root, target_sum)
print(result)  # Output: True (5 -> 4 -> 11 -> 2)
```

Binary Tree Traversals

Binary Tree Traversals refer to the methods of visiting all the nodes in a binary tree in a specific order. The three primary types of depth-first traversals are:

- **Inorder Traversal**: Left subtree, Root, Right subtree.
- **Preorder Traversal**: Root, Left subtree, Right subtree.
- **Postorder Traversal**: Left subtree, Right subtree, Root.

```python
class TreeNode:
    def __init__(self, value):
        self.value, self.left, self.right = value, None, None

class BinaryTree:
    def inorder(self, node):
        return self.inorder(node.left) + [node.value] + self.inorder(node.right) if node else []

    def preorder(self, node):
        return [node.value] + self.preorder(node.left) + self.preorder(node.right) if node else []

    def postorder(self, node):
        return self.postorder(node.left) + self.postorder(node.right) + [node.value] if node else []

# Example usage:
root = TreeNode(1)
root.left, root.right = TreeNode(2), TreeNode(3)
root.left.left, root.left.right = TreeNode(4), TreeNode(5)

tree = BinaryTree()
print("Inorder:", tree.inorder(root))    # Output: [4, 2, 5, 1, 3]
print("Preorder:", tree.preorder(root))
# Output: [1, 2, 4, 5, 3]
print("Postorder:", tree.postorder(root))
# Output: [4, 5, 2, 3, 1]
```

Diameter of Binary Tree

The diameter of a binary tree is the length of the longest path between any two nodes in the tree. This path may or may not pass through the root. The diameter can be calculated by determining the height of the left and right subtrees for each node and keeping track of the maximum diameter found during the traversal.

```python
class TreeNode:
    def __init__(self, value):
        self.value, self.left, self.right = value, None, None

class BinaryTree:
    def diameter(self, node):
        self.max_diameter = 0  # Initialize maximum diameter

        def height(n):
            if not n:
                return 0  # Base case: height of null is 0
            left_height = height(n.left)  # Height of left subtree
            right_height = height(n.right)  # Height of right subtree
            self.max_diameter = max(self.max_diameter, left_height + right_height)  # Update maximum diameter
            return max(left_height, right_height) + 1  # Return height

        height(node)  # Start the height calculation
        return self.max_diameter  # Return the maximum diameter

# Example usage:
root = TreeNode(1)
root.left, root.right = TreeNode(2), TreeNode(3)
root.left.left, root.left.right = TreeNode(4), TreeNode(5)

tree = BinaryTree()
```

```python
print(tree.diameter(root))
# Output: 3 (length of the path 4 -> 2 -> 1 -> 3)
```

Diff Views of Binary Tree

Different views of a binary tree provide distinct perspectives of the tree's structure. The most common views are:

1. **Left View**: The nodes visible when the tree is viewed from the left side.
2. **Right View**: The nodes visible when the tree is viewed from the right side.
3. **Top View**: The nodes visible from the top of the tree.
4. **Bottom View**: The nodes visible from the bottom of the tree.

```python
class TreeNode:
    def __init__(self, value):
        self.value, self.left, self.right = value, None, None

class BinaryTree:
    def left_view(self, node):
        result = []
        self._left_view_util(node, 0, result)
        return result

    def _left_view_util(self, node, level, result):
        if not node:
            return
        if level == len(result):  # First node at this level
            result.append(node.value)
        self._left_view_util(node.left, level + 1, result)   # Recur for left child
        self._left_view_util(node.right, level + 1, result)  # Recur for right child

    def right_view(self, node):
        result = []
        self._right_view_util(node, 0, result)
        return result

    def _right_view_util(self, node, level, result):
```

```python
        if not node:
            return
        if level == len(result):  # First node at this level
            result.append(node.value)
        self._right_view_util(node.right, level + 1, result)  # Recur for right child
        self._right_view_util(node.left, level + 1, result)  # Recur for left child

# Example usage:
root = TreeNode(1)
root.left, root.right = TreeNode(2), TreeNode(3)
root.left.left, root.left.right = TreeNode(4), TreeNode(5)
root.right.right = TreeNode(6)

tree = BinaryTree()
print("Left View:", tree.left_view(root))   # Output: [1, 2, 4]
print("Right View:", tree.right_view(root)) # Output: [1, 3, 6]
```

Distribute Coins

The "Distribute Coins" problem involves distributing a given number of coins to a set of piles according to specific rules. The most common variation is to ensure that each pile has at least one coin and to distribute the remaining coins as evenly as possible.

```python
def distribute_coins(n, k):
    if n < k:   # Not enough coins to give at least one to each pile
        return 0
    return comb(n - 1, k - 1)  # Combinations of (n-1) choose (k-1)

def comb(n, k):   # Calculate combinations nCk
    if k > n or k < 0:
        return 0
    if k == 0 or k == n:
        return 1
    k = min(k, n - k)  # Take advantage of symmetry
    c = 1
    for i in range(k):
        c = c * (n - i) // (i + 1)
    return c

# Example usage:
n = 10   # Total coins
k = 3    # Total piles
result = distribute_coins(n, k)
print(result)
# Output: 36 (ways to distribute 10 coins into 3 piles)
```

40

Fenwick Tree

A Fenwick Tree, also known as a Binary Indexed Tree (BIT), is a data structure that efficiently supports prefix sum queries and updates. It allows both operations in logarithmic time, making it suitable for scenarios where frequent updates and queries are needed, such as in cumulative frequency tables.

```python
class FenwickTree:
    def __init__(self, size):
        self.size = size
        self.tree = [0] * (size + 1)

    def update(self, index, value):
        while index <= self.size:
            self.tree[index] += value
            index += index & -index  # Move to the next index

    def query(self, index):
        total = 0
        while index > 0:
            total += self.tree[index]
            index -= index & -index  # Move to the parent index
        return total

# Example usage:
ft = FenwickTree(5)      # Create a Fenwick Tree of size 5
ft.update(1, 3)          # Add 3 to index 1
ft.update(2, 2)          # Add 2 to index 2
ft.update(3, 5)          # Add 5 to index 3
print(ft.query(3))       # Output: 10 (3 + 2 + 5)
print(ft.query(2))       # Output: 5 (3 + 2)
```

Floor and Ceiling

The "Floor and Ceiling" problem involves finding the floor and ceiling values of a given number in a sorted array. The floor is the largest number in the array that is less than or equal to the target value, while the ceiling is the smallest number that is greater than or equal to the target value.

```python
def find_floor_and_ceiling(arr, target):
    floor, ceiling = None, None
    for num in arr:
        if num <= target:
            floor = num  # Update floor if num is less than or equal to target
        if num >= target and ceiling is None:  # Update ceiling only once
            ceiling = num
    return floor, ceiling

# Example usage:
arr = [1, 2, 8, 10, 10, 12, 19]
target = 5
floor, ceiling = find_floor_and_ceiling(arr, target)
print(f"Floor: {floor}, Ceiling: {ceiling}")
# Output: Floor: 2, Ceiling: 8
```

Is Sorted

The "Is Sorted" problem involves checking whether a given list (or array) is sorted in either ascending or descending order. This can be useful for validating input data or optimizing algorithms that assume sorted input.

```python
def is_sorted(arr):
    ascending, descending = True, True
    for i in range(1, len(arr)):
        if arr[i] < arr[i - 1]:   # Check for ascending order
            ascending = False
        if arr[i] > arr[i - 1]:   # Check for descending order
            descending = False
    return ascending, descending

# Example usage:
arr = [1, 2, 3, 4, 5]
ascending, descending = is_sorted(arr)
print(f"Is Ascending: {ascending}, Is Descending: {descending}")
# Output: Is Ascending: True, Is Descending: False
```

Is Sum Tree

The "Is Sum Tree" problem involves determining whether a given binary tree is a Sum Tree. A binary tree is considered a Sum Tree if, for every node in the tree, the value of the node is equal to the sum of the values of its left and right children. This property must hold for all nodes in the tree.

```python
class TreeNode:
    def __init__(self, value):
        self.value = value
        self.left = None
        self.right = None

def is_sum_tree(node):
    if not node:  # An empty tree is a Sum Tree
        return 0
    if not node.left and not node.right:  # Leaf nodes
        return node.value

    left_sum = is_sum_tree(node.left)   # Recursively get left subtree sum
    right_sum = is_sum_tree(node.right)  # Recursively get right subtree sum

    if left_sum == -1 or right_sum == -1 or node.value != left_sum + right_sum:
        return -1  # Return -1 if it's not a Sum Tree

    return left_sum + right_sum + node.value  # Return the total sum of this subtree

# Example usage:
root = TreeNode(26)
root.left = TreeNode(10)
root.right = TreeNode(3)
root.left.left = TreeNode(4)
root.left.right = TreeNode(6)
root.right.right = TreeNode(3)

result = is_sum_tree(root)
```

```python
print(f"Is Sum Tree: {result != -1}")  # Output: Is Sum Tree: True
```

Lowest Common Ancestor

The Lowest Common Ancestor (LCA) of two nodes in a binary tree is the deepest node that is an ancestor of both nodes. It is commonly used in various tree-related algorithms and problems. The LCA can be efficiently found using a recursive approach or by maintaining parent pointers in the tree.

```python
class TreeNode:
    def __init__(self, value):
        self.value = value
        self.left = None
        self.right = None

def find_lca(root, n1, n2):
    if not root:
        return None
    if root.value == n1 or root.value == n2:
        return root
    
    left_lca = find_lca(root.left, n1, n2)
    right_lca = find_lca(root.right, n1, n2)
    
    if left_lca and right_lca:
        return root  # This is the LCA
    return left_lca if left_lca else right_lca  # Either one of the two

# Example usage:
root = TreeNode(1)
root.left = TreeNode(2)
root.right = TreeNode(3)
root.left.left = TreeNode(4)
root.left.right = TreeNode(5)

lca = find_lca(root, 4, 5)
print(f"LCA of 4 and 5: {lca.value}")
# Output: LCA of 4 and 5: 2
```

Maximum Fenwick Tree

A Maximum Fenwick Tree (or Maximum Binary Indexed Tree) is a data structure that supports efficient queries and updates for finding the maximum element within a range of an array. It is an extension of the standard Fenwick Tree (or Binary Indexed Tree) but is specifically designed to handle maximum queries instead of sum queries.

```python
class MaxFenwickTree:
    def __init__(self, size):
        self.size = size
        self.tree = [float('-inf')] * (size + 1)

    def update(self, index, value):
        while index <= self.size:
            self.tree[index] = max(self.tree[index], value)
            index += index & -index  # Move to the next index

    def query(self, index):
        max_val = float('-inf')
        while index > 0:
            max_val = max(max_val, self.tree[index])
            index -= index & -index  # Move to the parent index
        return max_val

    def range_max(self, left, right):
        return max(self.query(right), self.query(left - 1))

# Example usage:
fenwick_tree = MaxFenwickTree(5)
fenwick_tree.update(1, 10)
fenwick_tree.update(2, 20)
fenwick_tree.update(3, 15)

print(f"Maximum value between index 1 and 3: {fenwick_tree.range_max(1, 3)}")
# Output: 20
```

Number of Possible Binary Trees

The number of possible binary trees that can be formed with nnn nodes can be calculated using the **Catalan number**. The nthn^{th}nth Catalan number gives the count of distinct binary trees that can be formed using nnn distinct nodes. The formula for the nthn^{th}nth Catalan number is:

$$C(n) = \frac{1}{n+1}\binom{2n}{n} = \frac{(2n)!}{(n+1)!n!}$$

```python
def factorial(n):
    result = 1
    for i in range(2, n + 1):
        result *= i
    return result

def catalan_number(n):
    return factorial(2 * n) // (factorial(n + 1) * factorial(n))

# Example usage:
n = 3
print(f"Number of possible binary trees with {n} nodes: {catalan_number(n)}")
# Output: 5
```

Disjoint Set

A Disjoint Set, also known as Union-Find, is a data structure that maintains a collection of disjoint (non-overlapping) sets. It supports two primary operations: **Union**, which merges two sets, and **Find**, which determines which set a particular element belongs to. This structure is particularly useful in scenarios such as network connectivity, clustering, and Kruskal's algorithm for finding the Minimum Spanning Tree.

```python
class DisjointSet:
    def __init__(self, size):
        self.parent = list(range(size))  # Initially, each element is its own parent
        self.rank = [1] * size  # Used for union by rank

    def find(self, x):
        if self.parent[x] != x:
            self.parent[x] = self.find(self.parent[x])  # Path compression
        return self.parent[x]

    def union(self, x, y):
        rootX = self.find(x)
        rootY = self.find(y)

        if rootX != rootY:
            # Union by rank
            if self.rank[rootX] > self.rank[rootY]:
                self.parent[rootY] = rootX
            elif self.rank[rootX] < self.rank[rootY]:
                self.parent[rootX] = rootY
            else:
                self.parent[rootY] = rootX
                self.rank[rootX] += 1

# Example usage:
ds = DisjointSet(5)
ds.union(0, 1)
ds.union(1, 2)
```

```python
print("Find(0):", ds.find(0))   # Output: Find(0): 0
print("Find(1):", ds.find(1))   # Output: Find(1): 0
print("Find(2):", ds.find(2))   # Output: Find(2): 0
print("Find(3):", ds.find(3))   # Output: Find(3): 3 (3 is
its own set)
```

Hashing

Hashing is a technique used to uniquely identify data and facilitate fast data retrieval in data structures like hash tables. It involves converting input data (keys) into fixed-size values (hash codes or hash values) using a hash function. This process helps in storing, searching, and managing data efficiently. Hashing is commonly used in applications like databases, caches, and data integrity checks.

Bloom Filter

A Bloom Filter is a probabilistic data structure used to test whether an element is a member of a set. It allows for fast membership testing with the possibility of false positives but guarantees no false negatives. This means that if the filter indicates that an element is not in the set, it is definitely not present, but if it indicates that an element is in the set, there is a chance it might not be. Bloom Filters are useful in applications like spell-checking, network routing, and database query optimization, where space efficiency is crucial.

```python
import hashlib

class BloomFilter:
    def __init__(self, size, num_hashes):
        self.size = size
        self.num_hashes = num_hashes
        self.bit_array = [0] * size  # Initialize a bit array

    def _hashes(self, item):
        # Generate hash values for the item
        return [hashlib.md5(item.encode()).hexdigest(),
                hashlib.sha1(item.encode()).hexdigest(),
                hashlib.sha256(item.encode()).hexdigest()]

    def _get_indices(self, item):
        # Get indices based on hash values
        return [int(h, 16) % self.size for h in self._hashes(item)]

    def add(self, item):
        # Set bits in the bit array for the item
        for index in self._get_indices(item):
            self.bit_array[index] = 1

    def contains(self, item):
        # Check if the bits are set for the item
        return all(self.bit_array[index] for index in self._get_indices(item))

# Example usage:
```

```python
bloom = BloomFilter(size=100, num_hashes=3)
bloom.add("hello")
bloom.add("world")

print("Contains 'hello':", bloom.contains("hello"))  # Output: True
print("Contains 'world':", bloom.contains("world"))  # Output: True
print("Contains 'python':", bloom.contains("python"))  # Output: False (probabilistic)
```

Double Hash

Double Hashing is a technique used in open-addressing hash tables to resolve collisions by applying a second hash function when the first results in a collision. Unlike linear or quadratic probing, double hashing uses two hash functions to calculate the probe sequence, which ensures better distribution of values across the hash table. The key idea is that the second hash function provides an offset that varies for each key, reducing clustering and minimizing collisions.

```python
class DoubleHashTable:
    def __init__(self, size):
        self.size = size
        self.table = [None] * size
        self.used = [False] * size  # Track occupied slots

    def _primary_hash(self, key):
        return key % self.size   # Primary hash function

    def _secondary_hash(self, key):
        return 1 + (key % (self.size - 1))  # Secondary hash function

    def insert(self, key, value):
        index = self._primary_hash(key)
        step_size = self._secondary_hash(key)

        while self.used[index]:  # Find next free slot using double hashing
            index = (index + step_size) % self.size

        self.table[index] = (key, value)
        self.used[index] = True

    def search(self, key):
        index = self._primary_hash(key)
        step_size = self._secondary_hash(key)
        start_index = index

        while self.used[index]:
```

54

```python
            if self.table[index] and self.table[index][0] == key:
                return self.table[index][1]  # Key found, return value
            index = (index + step_size) % self.size
            if index == start_index:
                break  # If we've looped back to the start, stop search

        return None  # Key not found

# Example usage:
hash_table = DoubleHashTable(7)
hash_table.insert(10, 'A')
hash_table.insert(20, 'B')
hash_table.insert(15, 'C')
hash_table.insert(7, 'D')

print("Search key 10:", hash_table.search(10))  # Output: A
print("Search key 20:", hash_table.search(20))  # Output: B
print("Search key 7:", hash_table.search(7))    # Output: D
print("Search key 99:", hash_table.search(99))  # Output: None
```

Hash Map

A Hash Map, also known as a Hash Table, is a data structure that implements an associative array, allowing for efficient key-value pair storage and retrieval. It uses a hash function to compute an index (or hash code) into an array of buckets or slots, from which the desired value can be found. Hash Maps provide average-case constant time complexity ($O(1)$) for insertion, deletion, and search operations, making them a popular choice for implementing dictionaries and caches.

```python
class HashMap:
    def __init__(self, size=10):
        self.size = size
        self.table = [[] for _ in range(size)]  # Initialize buckets

    def _hash(self, key):
        return hash(key) % self.size  # Hash function to compute index

    def insert(self, key, value):
        index = self._hash(key)
        for i, (k, v) in enumerate(self.table[index]):
            if k == key:
                self.table[index][i] = (key, value)  # Update existing key
                return
        self.table[index].append((key, value))  # Insert new key-value pair

    def search(self, key):
        index = self._hash(key)
        for k, v in self.table[index]:
            if k == key:
                return v  # Key found, return value
        return None  # Key not found

    def delete(self, key):
        index = self._hash(key)
        for i, (k, v) in enumerate(self.table[index]):
            if k == key:
```

```python
                del self.table[index][i]  # Remove key-value pair
                return True
        return False  # Key not found

# Example usage:
hash_map = HashMap()
hash_map.insert("apple", 1)
hash_map.insert("banana", 2)
hash_map.insert("orange", 3)

print("Search apple:", hash_map.search("apple"))  # Output: 1
print("Search banana:", hash_map.search("banana"))  # Output: 2
print("Search grape:", hash_map.search("grape"))  # Output: None

hash_map.delete("banana")
print("Search banana after deletion:", hash_map.search("banana"))  # Output: None
```

Hash Table

A Hash Table is a data structure that implements an associative array, allowing for efficient storage and retrieval of key-value pairs. It uses a hash function to compute an index (or hash code) into an array of buckets or slots, where the values are stored. Hash Tables provide average-case constant time complexity (O(1)) for insertions, deletions, and lookups, making them a highly efficient choice for implementing dictionaries and caching mechanisms. Collisions, which occur when multiple keys hash to the same index, can be resolved using techniques like chaining or open addressing.

```python
class HashTable:
    def __init__(self, size=10):
        self.size = size
        self.table = [[] for _ in range(size)]  # Initialize buckets

    def _hash(self, key):
        return hash(key) % self.size  # Hash function to compute index

    def insert(self, key, value):
        index = self._hash(key)
        for i, (k, v) in enumerate(self.table[index]):
            if k == key:
                self.table[index][i] = (key, value)  # Update existing key
                return
        self.table[index].append((key, value))  # Insert new key-value pair

    def search(self, key):
        index = self._hash(key)
        for k, v in self.table[index]:
            if k == key:
                return v  # Key found, return value
        return None  # Key not found

    def delete(self, key):
        index = self._hash(key)
        for i, (k, v) in enumerate(self.table[index]):
```

```python
            if k == key:
                del self.table[index][i]  # Remove key-value pair
                return True
        return False  # Key not found

# Example usage:
hash_table = HashTable()
hash_table.insert("apple", 1)
hash_table.insert("banana", 2)
hash_table.insert("orange", 3)

print("Search apple:", hash_table.search("apple"))  # Output: 1
print("Search banana:", hash_table.search("banana"))  # Output: 2
print("Search grape:", hash_table.search("grape"))  # Output: None

hash_table.delete("banana")
print("Search banana after deletion:", hash_table.search("banana"))  # Output: None
```

Hash Table with Linked List

A Hash Table with Linked List is a variation of the standard hash table that uses linked lists to handle collisions. Each slot (or bucket) in the hash table contains a linked list of entries that hash to the same index. This approach allows for efficient storage and retrieval of key-value pairs while maintaining the average-case time complexity of O(1) for insertions, deletions, and lookups. When a collision occurs, the new entry is simply added to the linked list at the appropriate index.

```python
class Node:
    def __init__(self, key, value):
        self.key = key
        self.value = value
        self.next = None  # Pointer to the next node in the linked list

class HashTable:
    def __init__(self, size=10):
        self.size = size
        self.table = [None] * size  # Initialize buckets as None

    def _hash(self, key):
        return hash(key) % self.size  # Hash function to compute index

    def insert(self, key, value):
        index = self._hash(key)
        new_node = Node(key, value)

        if self.table[index] is None:
            self.table[index] = new_node  # No collision, insert directly
        else:
            # Collision occurred; insert at the beginning of the linked list
            new_node.next = self.table[index]
            self.table[index] = new_node

    def search(self, key):
```

```python
        index = self._hash(key)
        current = self.table[index]
        while current:
            if current.key == key:
                return current.value  # Key found, return value
            current = current.next  # Move to the next node
        return None  # Key not found

    def delete(self, key):
        index = self._hash(key)
        current = self.table[index]
        prev = None

        while current:
            if current.key == key:
                if prev:
                    prev.next = current.next  # Bypass the current node
                else:
                    self.table[index] = current.next  # Remove head node
                return True  # Key successfully deleted
            prev = current
            current = current.next
        return False  # Key not found

# Example usage:
hash_table = HashTable()
hash_table.insert("apple", 1)
hash_table.insert("banana", 2)
hash_table.insert("orange", 3)
hash_table.insert("banana", 4)  # Updating value for existing key

print("Search apple:", hash_table.search("apple"))  # Output: 1
print("Search banana:", hash_table.search("banana"))  # Output: 4
```

```python
print("Search grape:", hash_table.search("grape"))   # 
Output: None

hash_table.delete("banana")
print("Search banana after deletion:", 
hash_table.search("banana"))   # Output: None
```

Quadratic Probing

Quadratic Probing is a collision resolution technique used in open addressing hash tables. When a collision occurs (i.e., when two keys hash to the same index), quadratic probing finds the next available slot by checking positions at increasing intervals based on a quadratic function. This helps to reduce clustering, which can occur with linear probing, making it more efficient for certain scenarios. The formula for the probe sequence is typically defined as:

$$\text{index} = (h(key) + c_1^2 + c_2^2 + \ldots) \mod \text{table size}$$

where c1,c2,...c_1, c_2, \ldotsc1,c2,... are integers representing the probe count.

```python
class QuadraticProbingHashTable:
    def __init__(self, size=10):
        self.size = size
        self.table = [None] * size

    def _hash(self, key):
        return hash(key) % self.size   # Basic hash function

    def insert(self, key, value):
        index = self._hash(key)
        for i in range(self.size):
            new_index = (index + i * i) % self.size   # Quadratic probing
            if self.table[new_index] is None or self.table[new_index][0] == key:
                self.table[new_index] = (key, value)   # Insert key-value pair
                return

    def search(self, key):
        index = self._hash(key)
        for i in range(self.size):
            new_index = (index + i * i) % self.size
            if self.table[new_index] is None:
                break   # Key not found
            if self.table[new_index][0] == key:
```

```python
            return self.table[new_index][1]  # Return value
        return None  # Key not found

    def delete(self, key):
        index = self._hash(key)
        for i in range(self.size):
            new_index = (index + i * i) % self.size
            if self.table[new_index] is None:
                return False  # Key not found
            if self.table[new_index][0] == key:
                self.table[new_index] = None  # Remove key-value pair
                return True
        return False  # Key not found

# Example usage:
hash_table = QuadraticProbingHashTable()
hash_table.insert("apple", 1)
hash_table.insert("banana", 2)
hash_table.insert("orange", 3)
hash_table.insert("banana", 4)  # Updating value for existing key

print("Search apple:", hash_table.search("apple"))  # Output: 1
print("Search banana:", hash_table.search("banana"))  # Output: 4
print("Search grape:", hash_table.search("grape"))  # Output: None

hash_table.delete("banana")
print("Search banana after deletion:", hash_table.search("banana"))  # Output: None
```

Heap

A **heap** is a specialized tree-based data structure that satisfies the heap property. In a max heap, for any given node NNN, the value of NNN is greater than or equal to the values of its children, which means the largest element is at the root. Conversely, in a min heap, the value of NNN is less than or equal to the values of its children, ensuring the smallest element is at the root. Heaps are commonly used to implement priority queues, where the highest or lowest priority element can be efficiently retrieved.

```python
class MinHeap:
    def __init__(self):
        self.heap = []

    def insert(self, key):
        self.heap.append(key)  # Add the new key at the end
        self._bubble_up(len(self.heap) - 1)  # Bubble up to maintain heap property

    def _bubble_up(self, index):
        parent = (index - 1) // 2
        if index > 0 and self.heap[index] < self.heap[parent]:
            self.heap[index], self.heap[parent] = self.heap[parent], self.heap[index]  # Swap
            self._bubble_up(parent)  # Recur for the parent

    def extract_min(self):
        if not self.heap:
            return None
        if len(self.heap) == 1:
            return self.heap.pop()  # Remove and return the root
        root = self.heap[0]
        self.heap[0] = self.heap.pop()  # Move the last element to the root
        self._bubble_down(0)  # Bubble down to maintain heap property
        return root
```

```python
    def _bubble_down(self, index):
        smallest = index
        left = 2 * index + 1
        right = 2 * index + 2

        if left < len(self.heap) and self.heap[left] < self.heap[smallest]:
            smallest = left
        if right < len(self.heap) and self.heap[right] < self.heap[smallest]:
            smallest = right
        if smallest != index:
            self.heap[index], self.heap[smallest] = self.heap[smallest], self.heap[index]  # Swap
            self._bubble_down(smallest)  # Recur for the smallest child

    def get_min(self):
        return self.heap[0] if self.heap else None  # Return the root element

# Example usage:
min_heap = MinHeap()
min_heap.insert(3)
min_heap.insert(1)
min_heap.insert(4)
min_heap.insert(2)

print("Minimum element:", min_heap.get_min())  # Output: 1
print("Extracted minimum:", min_heap.extract_min())  # Output: 1
print("New minimum after extraction:", min_heap.get_min())  # Output: 2
```

Binomial Heap

A **Binomial Heap** is a collection of binomial trees that satisfies the properties of a min-heap or max-heap. It is a more advanced data structure compared to simple binary heaps, allowing for more efficient merging of heaps. A binomial heap is made up of a set of binomial trees, where each tree is an ordered tree defined recursively. Binomial heaps support operations like insertion, deletion, and merging efficiently, making them suitable for applications that require frequent merging of heaps.

```python
class Node:
    def __init__(self, key):
        self.key = key
        self.degree = 0
        self.parent = None
        self.child = None
        self.sibling = None

class BinomialHeap:
    def __init__(self):
        self.head = None

    def _merge(self, h1, h2):
        if not h1 or not h2:
            return h1 or h2

        # Merging two binomial trees
        if h1.degree <= h2.degree:
            h1.sibling = self._merge(h1.sibling, h2)
            return h1
        else:
            h2.sibling = self._merge(h1, h2.sibling)
            return h2

    def _link(self, y, z):
        y.parent = z
        y.sibling = z.child
        z.child = y
        z.degree += 1

    def insert(self, key):
```

```python
        new_heap = BinomialHeap()
        new_heap.head = Node(key)
        self.head = self._merge(self.head, new_heap.head)

    def find_min(self):
        min_node = self.head
        current = self.head
        while current:
            if current.key < min_node.key:
                min_node = current
            current = current.sibling
        return min_node

    def extract_min(self):
        if not self.head:
            return None

        min_node = self.find_min()
        if min_node == self.head:
            self.head = self.head.sibling
        else:
            current = self.head
            while current.sibling != min_node:
                current = current.sibling
            current.sibling = min_node.sibling

        # Reverse the children of min_node
        child = min_node.child
        min_node.child = None
        while child:
            next_child = child.sibling
            child.sibling = self.head
            self.head = child
            child = next_child

        return min_node.key

# Example usage:
binomial_heap = BinomialHeap()
```

```python
binomial_heap.insert(3)
binomial_heap.insert(1)
binomial_heap.insert(4)
binomial_heap.insert(2)

print("Minimum element:", binomial_heap.find_min().key)  # Output: 1
print("Extracted minimum:", binomial_heap.extract_min())  # Output: 1
print("New minimum after extraction:", binomial_heap.find_min().key)  # Output: 2
```

Heap Generic

A generic heap is a flexible data structure that can manage elements of any data type while adhering to the heap property (either min-heap or max-heap). By using generics, this heap can be utilized with different data types without the need to rewrite the implementation for each type. This is particularly useful in programming languages that support generics or templates, allowing for type-safe operations and code reusability.

```python
import heapq

class GenericMinHeap:
    def __init__(self):
        self.heap = []

    def insert(self, item):
        heapq.heappush(self.heap, item)  # Add item to the heap

    def extract_min(self):
        return heapq.heappop(self.heap) if self.heap else None  # Remove and return the smallest item

    def get_min(self):
        return self.heap[0] if self.heap else None  # Return the smallest item without removing

    def is_empty(self):
        return len(self.heap) == 0  # Check if the heap is empty

# Example usage:
min_heap = GenericMinHeap()
min_heap.insert(3)
min_heap.insert(1)
min_heap.insert(4)
min_heap.insert(2)

print("Minimum element:", min_heap.get_min())  # Output: 1
print("Extracted minimum:", min_heap.extract_min())  # Output: 1
```

```python
print("New minimum after extraction:",
min_heap.get_min())   # Output: 2

# Working with different data types
min_heap.insert("apple")
min_heap.insert("banana")
min_heap.insert("cherry")

print("Minimum string element:", min_heap.get_min())  # Output: 2 (since strings are not sorted with numbers)
```

Max Heap

A Max Heap is a complete binary tree where the value of each node is greater than or equal to the values of its children. This property makes it suitable for implementing priority queues, where the highest priority element is always accessible at the root. In a max heap, insertion and deletion operations are performed while maintaining the heap property.

```python
class MaxHeap:
    def __init__(self):
        self.heap = []

    def insert(self, item):
        self.heap.append(item)  # Add item to the end
        self._heapify_up(len(self.heap) - 1)  # Maintain heap property

    def _heapify_up(self, index):
        parent = (index - 1) // 2
        if index > 0 and self.heap[index] > self.heap[parent]:
            self.heap[index], self.heap[parent] = self.heap[parent], self.heap[index]  # Swap
            self._heapify_up(parent)  # Recur for parent

    def extract_max(self):
        if not self.heap:
            return None
        max_value = self.heap[0]
        last_value = self.heap.pop()  # Remove last element
        if self.heap:
            self.heap[0] = last_value  # Move last to root
            self._heapify_down(0)  # Maintain heap property
        return max_value

    def _heapify_down(self, index):
        largest = index
        left = 2 * index + 1
        right = 2 * index + 2
```

```python
            if left < len(self.heap) and self.heap[left] > self.heap[largest]:
                largest = left
            if right < len(self.heap) and self.heap[right] > self.heap[largest]:
                largest = right
            if largest != index:
                self.heap[index], self.heap[largest] = self.heap[largest], self.heap[index]  # Swap
                self._heapify_down(largest)  # Recur for largest

    def get_max(self):
        return self.heap[0] if self.heap else None  # Return max without removing

    def is_empty(self):
        return len(self.heap) == 0  # Check if the heap is empty

# Example usage:
max_heap = MaxHeap()
max_heap.insert(3)
max_heap.insert(1)
max_heap.insert(4)
max_heap.insert(2)

print("Maximum element:", max_heap.get_max())  # Output: 4
print("Extracted maximum:", max_heap.extract_max())  # Output: 4
print("New maximum after extraction:", max_heap.get_max())  # Output: 3
```

Min Heap

A Min Heap is a complete binary tree where the value of each node is less than or equal to the values of its children. This property allows the minimum element to be accessed quickly at the root, making it ideal for implementing priority queues that prioritize lower values. Operations such as insertion and deletion are performed while maintaining the heap property.

```python
class MinHeap:
    def __init__(self):
        self.heap = []

    def insert(self, item):
        self.heap.append(item)  # Add item to the end
        self._heapify_up(len(self.heap) - 1)  # Maintain heap property

    def _heapify_up(self, index):
        parent = (index - 1) // 2
        if index > 0 and self.heap[index] < self.heap[parent]:
            self.heap[index], self.heap[parent] = self.heap[parent], self.heap[index]  # Swap
            self._heapify_up(parent)  # Recur for parent

    def extract_min(self):
        if not self.heap:
            return None
        min_value = self.heap[0]
        last_value = self.heap.pop()  # Remove last element
        if self.heap:
            self.heap[0] = last_value  # Move last to root
            self._heapify_down(0)  # Maintain heap property
        return min_value

    def _heapify_down(self, index):
        smallest = index
        left = 2 * index + 1
        right = 2 * index + 2
```

```python
        if left < len(self.heap) and self.heap[left] < self.heap[smallest]:
            smallest = left
        if right < len(self.heap) and self.heap[right] < self.heap[smallest]:
            smallest = right
        if smallest != index:
            self.heap[index], self.heap[smallest] = self.heap[smallest], self.heap[index]  # Swap
            self._heapify_down(smallest)  # Recur for smallest

    def get_min(self):
        return self.heap[0] if self.heap else None  # Return min without removing

    def is_empty(self):
        return len(self.heap) == 0  # Check if the heap is empty

# Example usage:
min_heap = MinHeap()
min_heap.insert(3)
min_heap.insert(1)
min_heap.insert(4)
min_heap.insert(2)

print("Minimum element:", min_heap.get_min())  # Output: 1
print("Extracted minimum:", min_heap.extract_min())  # Output: 1
print("New minimum after extraction:", min_heap.get_min())  # Output: 2
```

Randomized Heap

A Randomized Heap is a data structure that integrates randomization techniques with heap properties to optimize operations such as insertion and extraction. This structure helps maintain efficient performance for managing a collection of elements, particularly in scenarios where the order of elements needs to be dynamically adjusted. Randomized heaps can provide better average-case time complexity compared to traditional heaps, especially in operations that benefit from random distribution.

```python
import random

class RandomizedHeap:
    def __init__(self):
        self.heap = []

    def insert(self, item):
        self.heap.append(item)  # Insert at the end
        self._heapify_up(len(self.heap) - 1)  # Restore heap property

    def _heapify_up(self, idx):
        parent = (idx - 1) // 2
        if idx > 0 and self.heap[idx] < self.heap[parent]:
            self.heap[idx], self.heap[parent] = self.heap[parent], self.heap[idx]  # Swap
            self._heapify_up(parent)  # Recur upwards

    def extract_min(self):
        if not self.heap:
            return None
        min_value = self.heap[0]
        last_value = self.heap.pop()  # Remove last element
        if self.heap:
            self.heap[0] = last_value  # Replace root with last
            self._heapify_down(0)  # Restore heap property
        return min_value

    def _heapify_down(self, idx):
```

```python
            smallest = idx
        left, right = 2 * idx + 1, 2 * idx + 2
            if left < len(self.heap) and self.heap[left] < self.heap[smallest]:
            smallest = left
         if right < len(self.heap) and self.heap[right] < self.heap[smallest]:
            smallest = right
        if smallest != idx:
                self.heap[idx], self.heap[smallest] = self.heap[smallest], self.heap[idx]  # Swap
            self._heapify_down(smallest)  # Recur downwards

    def random_merge(self, other):
        self.heap += other.heap  # Combine heaps
        random.shuffle(self.heap)  # Shuffle for randomness
        self.build_heap()  # Restore heap property

    def build_heap(self):
        for i in range(len(self.heap) // 2 - 1, -1, -1):
            self._heapify_down(i  # Restore properties

# Example usage:
randomized_heap = RandomizedHeap()
for num in [5, 1, 3, 4, 2]:
    randomized_heap.insert(num)

print("Minimum:", randomized_heap.extract_min())  # Output: 1
print("Current Heap:", randomized_heap.heap)  # Output: Remaining elements
```

Skew Heap

A Skew Heap is a type of binary heap that allows for a more flexible merging process. Unlike traditional binary heaps, where the structure is fixed, skew heaps are self-adjusting. They utilize a simple strategy for merging heaps that allows for efficient insertions and deletions while maintaining the heap properties. The main advantage of skew heaps is their efficient merging operation, making them suitable for applications like priority queues where merging heaps is a frequent operation.

```python
class SkewHeapNode:
    def __init__(self, key):
        self.key = key
        self.left = None
        self.right = None

class SkewHeap:
    def merge(self, h1, h2):
        if not h1: return h2
        if not h2: return h1

        # Ensure h1 has the smaller root
        if h1.key > h2.key:
            h1, h2 = h2, h1

        # Merge right subtree with h2
        h1.right = self.merge(h1.right, h2)
        # Swap left and right children
        h1.left, h1.right = h1.right, h1.left

        return h1

    def insert(self, root, key):
        new_node = SkewHeapNode(key)
        return self.merge(root, new_node)

    def extract_min(self, root):
        if not root:
            return None
        min_value = root.key
        root = self.merge(root.left, root.right)
```

```python
        return min_value, root  # Return min value and new root

# Example usage:
skew_heap = SkewHeap()
root = None
for num in [5, 1, 3, 4, 2]:
    root = skew_heap.insert(root, num)

min_value, root = skew_heap.extract_min(root)
print("Minimum:", min_value)  # Output: 1
print("Current Root:", root.key)  # Output: New root after extraction
```

Kdtree

A **KD-Tree** is a data structure used for organizing points in a k-dimensional space. It is particularly useful for applications that require multidimensional searching, such as range searches and nearest neighbor searches. KD-Trees recursively partition the space into hyperplanes, allowing for efficient querying of points based on their coordinates.

Build Kdtree

Building a KD-Tree involves organizing points in a k-dimensional space by recursively partitioning the data along different dimensions. The process begins by selecting the median of the points along the current dimension as the root node, then recursively doing the same for the left and right halves of the data. This results in a balanced tree structure that facilitates efficient multidimensional queries.

```python
class KDNode:
    def __init__(self, point, axis):
        self.point = point   # The k-dimensional point
        self.left = None     # Left child
        self.right = None    # Right child
        self.axis = axis     # Axis for this node

class KDTree:
    def build(self, points, depth=0):
        if not points:
            return None
        k = len(points[0])   # Number of dimensions
        axis = depth % k     # Current axis
        points.sort(key=lambda x: x[axis])   # Sort points by axis
        median = len(points) // 2   # Choose median
        node = KDNode(points[median], axis)   # Create node
        # Recursively build left and right subtrees
        node.left = self.build(points[:median], depth + 1)
        node.right = self.build(points[median + 1:], depth + 1)
        return node

# Example usage:
points = [(7, 2), (5, 4), (9, 6), (2, 3), (4, 7), (8, 1)]
kd_tree = KDTree()
root = kd_tree.build(points)

# Function to print the KD-Tree (for demonstration purposes)
def print_kd_tree(node, depth=0):
```

```python
    if node is not None:
        print_kd_tree(node.left, depth + 1)
        print(' ' * depth * 4, node.point)
        print_kd_tree(node.right, depth + 1)

print_kd_tree(root)    # Output the KD-Tree structure
```

Hypercube Points

A hypercube is a generalization of a square (2D) and cube (3D) to higher dimensions. In an n-dimensional space, a hypercube consists of 2n2^n2n vertices, each represented by an n-tuple of binary values (0s and 1s). This means that each vertex corresponds to a unique combination of coordinates in n-dimensional space. Generating the vertices of a hypercube can be useful in various applications, including computer graphics, optimization problems, and multidimensional data analysis.

```python
def generate_hypercube_points(n):
    return [[(i >> j) & 1 for j in range(n)] for i in range(1 << n)]

# Example usage:
n = 3  # Dimension of the hypercube
points = generate_hypercube_points(n)
print("Hypercube Points (3D):")
for point in points:
    print(point)

# Output: Points of a 3D hypercube
```

Kd Node

A KD Node is a fundamental building block of a KD-Tree (k-dimensional tree), which is a data structure used for organizing points in a k-dimensional space. Each KD Node contains a point and two children (left and right) that represent subtrees of points. The KD-Tree allows for efficient range searches and nearest neighbor searches by recursively dividing the space along different dimensions.

```python
class KDNode:
    def __init__(self, point, axis):
        self.point = point  # k-dimensional point (list or tuple)
        self.left = None    # Left child
        self.right = None   # Right child
        self.axis = axis    # Axis for partitioning (dimension)

# Example usage:
# Creating a KD Node for a point in 3D space
node = KDNode(point=[2, 3, 4], axis=0)

print("KD Node Point:", node.point)      # Output: [2, 3, 4]
print("Partitioning Axis:", node.axis)   # Output: 0
```

Nearest Neighbour Search

Nearest Neighbor Search (NNS) is a common problem in machine learning and data analysis, where the goal is to find the closest point(s) to a given query point in a dataset. This search is particularly important in various applications such as classification, clustering, and recommendation systems. Efficient algorithms, such as KD-Trees or Ball Trees, are often used to speed up the search process in multi-dimensional spaces.

```python
from scipy.spatial import KDTree

def nearest_neighbor_search(points, query_point):
    tree = KDTree(points)  # Build the KD-Tree
    distance, index = tree.query(query_point)  # Query the nearest neighbor
    return points[index], distance  # Return the nearest point and distance

# Example usage:
points = [[1, 2], [3, 4], [5, 6], [7, 8]]
query_point = [4, 5]
nearest_point, nearest_distance = nearest_neighbor_search(points, query_point)

print("Nearest Point:", nearest_point)  # Output: [3, 4]
print("Distance:", nearest_distance)    # Output: 1.4142135623730951
```

Linked List

A linked list is a linear data structure consisting of a sequence of elements, where each element (or node) contains a reference (or link) to the next element in the sequence. Unlike arrays, linked lists do not require contiguous memory allocation, allowing for efficient insertion and deletion of elements. Linked lists can be singly linked (each node points to the next node) or doubly linked (each node points to both the next and previous nodes).

Floyds Cycle Detection

Floyd's Cycle Detection, also known as the Tortoise and Hare algorithm, is a classic algorithm used to detect cycles in a linked list. It uses two pointers, one moving slowly (the tortoise) and the other moving faster (the hare). If there is a cycle in the linked list, the two pointers will eventually meet; otherwise, the faster pointer will reach the end of the list.

```python
class Node:
    def __init__(self, data):
        self.data = data
        self.next = None

def has_cycle(head):
    tortoise = hare = head
    while hare and hare.next:
        tortoise = tortoise.next         # Move tortoise by 1
        hare = hare.next.next            # Move hare by 2
        if tortoise == hare:             # Cycle detected
            return True
    return False                         # No cycle

# Example usage:
head = Node(1)
second = Node(2)
third = Node(3)
fourth = Node(4)

head.next = second
second.next = third
third.next = fourth
fourth.next = second  # Creating a cycle

print(has_cycle(head))   # Output: True

fourth.next = None   # Removing the cycle
print(has_cycle(head))   # Output: False
```

From Sequence

Generating a sequence based on a specified pattern involves creating a series of numbers that follow a particular rule or mathematical function. This can range from simple arithmetic sequences to more complex patterns based on recurrence relations. Below is an example of generating a sequence of Fibonacci numbers.

```python
def fibonacci(n):
    seq = [0, 1]
    for _ in range(2, n):
        seq.append(seq[-1] + seq[-2])  # Append the sum of the last two numbers
    return seq[:n]

# Example usage:
print(fibonacci(10))
# Output: [0, 1, 1, 2, 3, 5, 8, 13, 21, 34]
```

Has Loop

Detecting a loop (or cycle) in a linked list is crucial to prevent infinite loops during traversal. One efficient way to achieve this is by using Floyd's Cycle Detection Algorithm (Tortoise and Hare). The idea is to use two pointers that move at different speeds through the list. If they meet, a loop exists.

```python
class Node:
    def __init__(self, data):
        self.data = data
        self.next = None

def has_loop(head):
    slow = fast = head
    while fast and fast.next:
        slow = slow.next          # Move slow by 1
        fast = fast.next.next     # Move fast by 2
        if slow == fast:          # Loop detected
            return True
    return False                  # No loop

# Example usage:
head = Node(1)
second = Node(2)
third = Node(3)
fourth = Node(4)

head.next = second
second.next = third
third.next = fourth
fourth.next = second  # Creating a loop

print(has_loop(head))   # Output: True

fourth.next = None  # Removing the loop
print(has_loop(head))   # Output: False
```

Middle Element of Linked List

To find the middle element of a linked list, we can use the two-pointer technique, commonly known as the "slow and fast pointer" approach. This method efficiently determines the middle node by moving one pointer (slow) one step at a time and another pointer (fast) two steps at a time. When the fast pointer reaches the end of the list, the slow pointer will be at the middle.

```python
class Node:
    def __init__(self, data):
        self.data = data
        self.next = None

def find_middle(head):
    slow = fast = head

    while fast and fast.next:
        slow = slow.next          # Move slow pointer by one
        fast = fast.next.next     # Move fast pointer by two

    return slow  # slow pointer will be at the middle node

# Example usage:
head = Node(1)
head.next = Node(2)
head.next.next = Node(3)
head.next.next.next = Node(4)
head.next.next.next.next = Node(5)

middle_node = find_middle(head)
print(middle_node.data)   # Output: 3
```

Print Reverse

To print a linked list in reverse order, we can utilize recursion. By leveraging the call stack, we can visit each node in the list and print its data after the recursive calls return, effectively reversing the order of output.

```python
class Node:
    def __init__(self, data):
        self.data = data
        self.next = None

def print_reverse(head):
    if head is None:
        return
    print_reverse(head.next)   # Recursive call
    print(head.data, end=" ")  # Print after the recursive call

# Example usage:
head = Node(1)
head.next = Node(2)
head.next.next = Node(3)
head.next.next.next = Node(4)
head.next.next.next.next = Node(5)

print_reverse(head)   # Output: 5 4 3 2 1
```

Swap Nodes

Swapping nodes in pairs in a linked list involves rearranging the nodes such that every two adjacent nodes are swapped. If the linked list has an odd number of nodes, the last node remains unchanged.

```python
class ListNode:
    def __init__(self, val=0, next=None):
        self.val = val
        self.next = next

class Solution:
    def swapPairs(self, head: ListNode) -> ListNode:
        dummy = ListNode(0, head)
        prev = dummy

        while prev.next and prev.next.next:
            first = prev.next
            second = first.next
            # Swapping nodes
            prev.next, first.next, second.next = second, second.next, first

            prev = first  # Move prev to the next pair

        return dummy.next

# Example usage:
head = ListNode(1, ListNode(2, ListNode(3, ListNode(4))))
solution = Solution()
swapped_head = solution.swapPairs(head)

# Output the swapped list
result = []
while swapped_head:
    result.append(swapped_head.val)
    swapped_head = swapped_head.next

print(result)  # Output: [2, 1, 4, 3]
```

Queue

A queue is a linear data structure that follows the First In, First Out (FIFO) principle. This means that the first element added to the queue will be the first one to be removed. Queues are used in various applications, such as scheduling tasks, managing requests in web servers, and implementing breadth-first search (BFS) in graph algorithms.

Priority Queue Using List

A priority queue is an abstract data type that operates similarly to a regular queue but with an added feature: each element has a priority associated with it. In a priority queue, elements with higher priority are dequeued before elements with lower priority. This implementation uses a list to manage the elements, where the list is sorted based on the priority of the elements.

```python
class PriorityQueue:
    def __init__(self):
        self.elements = []

    def is_empty(self):
        return not self.elements

    def enqueue(self, item, priority):
        self.elements.append((item, priority))
        self.elements.sort(key=lambda x: x[1], reverse=True)  # Sort by priority

    def dequeue(self):
        return self.elements.pop(0)[0] if not self.is_empty() else None  # Remove highest priority

    def peek(self):
        return self.elements[0][0] if not self.is_empty() else None  # Return highest priority

# Example usage:
pq = PriorityQueue()
pq.enqueue("task1", 2)
pq.enqueue("task2", 1)
pq.enqueue("task3", 3)

print(pq.dequeue())   # Output: task3 (highest priority)
print(pq.peek())      # Output: task1 (next highest priority)
print(pq.is_empty())  # Output: False
```

Queue by List

A queue is a linear data structure that follows the First In First Out (FIFO) principle, meaning the first element added to the queue will be the first one to be removed. This implementation uses a list to manage the elements, allowing for enqueue (addition) and dequeue (removal) operations.

```python
class Queue:
    def __init__(self):
        self.items = []

    def is_empty(self):
        return not self.items

    def enqueue(self, item):
        self.items.append(item)  # Add item to the end of the list

    def dequeue(self):
        return self.items.pop(0) if not self.is_empty() else None  # Remove item from the front

    def peek(self):
        return self.items[0] if not self.is_empty() else None  # Get item from the front without removing

# Example usage:
queue = Queue()
queue.enqueue(1)
queue.enqueue(2)
queue.enqueue(3)

print(queue.dequeue())    # Output: 1
print(queue.peek())       # Output: 2
print(queue.is_empty())   # Output: False
```

Stacks

A stack is a linear data structure that follows the Last In First Out (LIFO) principle, meaning the last element added to the stack is the first one to be removed. Stacks are widely used in programming for various purposes, such as function calls, expression evaluation, and backtracking algorithms.

Balanced Parenthesis

The balanced parenthesis problem involves determining if the parentheses in a given expression are correctly matched and nested. A string containing parentheses is considered balanced if every opening parenthesis has a corresponding closing parenthesis in the correct order.

```python
def is_balanced(expression):
    stack = []  # Stack to hold opening parentheses
    mapping = {')': '(', '}': '{', ']': '['}  # Mapping for closing to opening parentheses
    
    for char in expression:
        if char in mapping.values():  # If it's an opening bracket
            stack.append(char)  # Push to stack
        elif char in mapping.keys():  # If it's a closing bracket
            if stack and stack[-1] == mapping[char]:  # Check for match
                stack.pop()  # Pop if matched
            else:
                return False  # Unmatched closing bracket
    return not stack  # Return True if stack is empty (balanced)

# Example usage:
expr1 = "{[()]}"
expr2 = "{[(])}"

print(is_balanced(expr1))  # Output: True
print(is_balanced(expr2))  # Output: False
```

Infix to Postfix Conversion

Infix expressions are the common arithmetic expressions where operators are placed between operands (e.g., `A + B`). However, computers prefer postfix expressions (or Reverse Polish Notation) where operators follow their operands (e.g., `A B +`). This conversion can be performed using the Shunting Yard algorithm developed by Edsger Dijkstra, which utilizes a stack to reorder the operators and operands.

```python
def infix_to_postfix(expression):
    precedence = {'+': 1, '-': 1, '*': 2, '/': 2, '^': 3}
    output = []
    stack = []
    
    for token in expression.split():
        if token.isalnum():  # Operand
            output.append(token)
        elif token in precedence:  # Operator
            while (stack and stack[-1] != '(' and
                    precedence[stack[-1]] >= precedence[token]):
                output.append(stack.pop())
            stack.append(token)
        elif token == '(':  # Left parenthesis
            stack.append(token)
        elif token == ')':  # Right parenthesis
            while stack and stack[-1] != '(':
                output.append(stack.pop())
            stack.pop()  # Pop the left parenthesis
    
    while stack:  # Pop all remaining operators
        output.append(stack.pop())
    
    return ' '.join(output)

# Example usage
infix_expr = "A + B * C - D"
print(infix_to_postfix(infix_expr))   # Output: A B C * + D -
```

Next Greater Element

The "Next Greater Element" problem involves finding the next greater element for each element in an array. For each element in the array, you need to determine the first element to its right that is greater than it. If no such element exists, you can use a placeholder (like -1).

```python
def next_greater_element(arr):
    stack, result = [], [-1] * len(arr)

    for i in range(len(arr)):
        while stack and arr[i] > arr[stack[-1]]:
            result[stack.pop()] = arr[i]
        stack.append(i)

    return result

# Example usage
arr = [4, 5, 2, 10, 8]
print(next_greater_element(arr))   # Output: [5, 10, 10, -1, -1]
```

Postfix Evaluation

Postfix evaluation, also known as Reverse Polish Notation (RPN), is a mathematical notation in which every operator follows all of its operands. It eliminates the need for parentheses to dictate order of operations. For example, the postfix expression 2 3 + evaluates to 5, while 2 3 * 4 + evaluates to 10.

```python
def evaluate_postfix(expression):
    stack = []

    for token in expression.split():
        if token.isdigit():  # If the token is an operand
            stack.append(int(token))
        else:  # The token is an operator
            b = stack.pop()
            a = stack.pop()
            if token == '+':
                stack.append(a + b)
            elif token == '-':
                stack.append(a - b)
            elif token == '*':
                stack.append(a * b)
            elif token == '/':
                stack.append(a // b)  # Use floor division for integers

    return stack[0] if stack else None

# Example usage
postfix_expr = "5 1 2 + 4 * + 3 -"
print(evaluate_postfix(postfix_expr))  # Output: 14
```

100

Prefix Evaluation

Prefix evaluation, also known as Polish Notation, is a mathematical notation in which every operator precedes its operands. This notation also eliminates the need for parentheses to define the order of operations. For example, the prefix expression + 2 3 evaluates to 5, while + * 2 3 4 evaluates to 10.

```python
def evaluate_prefix(expression):
    stack = []

    for token in reversed(expression.split()):
        if token.isdigit():  # If the token is an operand
            stack.append(int(token))
        else:  # The token is an operator
            a = stack.pop()
            b = stack.pop()
            if token == '+':
                stack.append(a + b)
            elif token == '-':
                stack.append(a - b)
            elif token == '*':
                stack.append(a * b)
            elif token == '/':
                stack.append(a // b)  # Use floor division for integers

    return stack[0] if stack else None

# Example usage
prefix_expr = "* + 2 3 4"
print(evaluate_prefix(prefix_expr))  # Output: 20
```

101

Stock Span Problem

The Stock Span Problem involves calculating the span of stock prices for a given number of days. The span of a stock's price on a given day is defined as the maximum number of consecutive days (up to that day) for which the price of the stock has been less than or equal to the price on that day. This problem can be efficiently solved using a stack.

```python
def calculate_span(prices):
    n = len(prices)
    span = [0] * n
    stack = []

    for i in range(n):
        while stack and prices[stack[-1]] <= prices[i]:
            stack.pop()
        span[i] = i + 1 if not stack else i - stack[-1]
        stack.append(i)

    return span

# Example usage
stock_prices = [100, 80, 60, 70, 60, 75, 85]
print(calculate_span(stock_prices))  # Output: [1, 1, 1, 2, 1, 4, 6]
```

Sorting Algorithms

Sorting algorithms are algorithms designed to arrange elements in a specific order, typically in ascending or descending order. They are fundamental in computer science and programming because they enable efficient data organization, which is crucial for searching, indexing, and other operations.

Bogo Sort

Bogo Sort (also known as Stupid Sort) is a highly inefficient sorting algorithm based on the generate-and-test paradigm. It repeatedly shuffles the list until it is sorted. Due to its nature, Bogo Sort has an average time complexity of $O((n+1)!)O((n+1)!)O((n+1)!)$, making it impractical for large arrays.

```python
import random

# Function to check if the array is sorted
def is_sorted(arr):
    for i in range(len(arr) - 1):
        if arr[i] > arr[i + 1]:
            return False
    return True

# Bogo Sort function
def bogo_sort(arr):
    attempts = 0
    while not is_sorted(arr):
        random.shuffle(arr)   # Shuffle the array
        attempts += 1
    return arr, attempts

# Example usage
arr = [3, 2, 5, 1, 4]
sorted_arr, attempts = bogo_sort(arr)
print("Sorted array:", sorted_arr)
print("Attempts taken:", attempts)
```

Bubble Sort

Bubble Sort is a simple sorting algorithm that repeatedly steps through the list, compares adjacent elements, and swaps them if they are in the wrong order. This process is repeated until the list is sorted. The largest unsorted element "bubbles" to its correct position at the end of each pass.

```python
def bubble_sort(arr):
    n = len(arr)
    # Traverse through all array elements
    for i in range(n):
        # Track if a swap happens
        swapped = False
        # Last i elements are already in place
        for j in range(0, n - i - 1):
            # Swap if the element found is greater than the next element
            if arr[j] > arr[j + 1]:
                arr[j], arr[j + 1] = arr[j + 1], arr[j]
                swapped = True
        # If no elements were swapped, the array is sorted
        if not swapped:
            break
    return arr

# Example usage
arr = [64, 34, 25, 12, 22, 11, 90]
sorted_arr = bubble_sort(arr)
print("Sorted array:", sorted_arr)
```

Counting Sort

Counting Sort is a non-comparison-based sorting algorithm that works well when the range of input values is known and limited. It counts the occurrences of each unique value and uses this count to place elements in their correct position in the sorted array. It is efficient for sorting integers within a limited range.

```python
def counting_sort(arr):
    if not arr:
        return arr

    # Find the maximum value in the array
    max_val = max(arr)

    # Create a count array and initialize it with zeros
    count = [0] * (max_val + 1)

    # Count the occurrences of each value in the array
    for num in arr:
        count[num] += 1

    # Build the sorted array
    sorted_arr = []
    for i, cnt in enumerate(count):
        sorted_arr.extend([i] * cnt)

    return sorted_arr

# Example usage
arr = [4, 2, 2, 8, 3, 3, 1]
sorted_arr = counting_sort(arr)
print("Sorted array:", sorted_arr)
```

Double Sort (Hybrid Sort Approach)

This approach combines two sorting algorithms, like Bubble Sort and Insertion Sort, to leverage the strengths of both. For example, we can first apply a simple sort like Bubble Sort and then use a more efficient algorithm like Insertion Sort for finer sorting.

```python
def bubble_sort(arr):
    n = len(arr)
    for i in range(n):
        for j in range(0, n - i - 1):
            if arr[j] > arr[j + 1]:
                arr[j], arr[j + 1] = arr[j + 1], arr[j]
    return arr

def insertion_sort(arr):
    for i in range(1, len(arr)):
        key = arr[i]
        j = i - 1
        while j >= 0 and arr[j] > key:
            arr[j + 1] = arr[j]
            j -= 1
        arr[j + 1] = key
    return arr

def double_sort(arr):
    # Apply Bubble Sort first
    bubble_sorted_arr = bubble_sort(arr.copy())
    
    # Apply Insertion Sort on the result of Bubble Sort
    sorted_arr = insertion_sort(bubble_sorted_arr)
    
    return sorted_arr

# Example usage
arr = [64, 34, 25, 12, 22, 11, 90]
sorted_arr = double_sort(arr)
print("Sorted array:", sorted_arr)
```

Dutch National Flag Sort

The algorithm works by partitioning the array into three sections based on the three distinct values, and then rearranging the elements so that each section contains only one of the three values. This is done using three pointers: `low`, `mid`, and `high`.

```python
def dutch_national_flag_sort(arr):
    low, mid, high = 0, 0, len(arr) - 1
    pivot = 1  # Assuming the values are 0, 1, and 2

    while mid <= high:
        if arr[mid] < pivot:
            arr[low], arr[mid] = arr[mid], arr[low]
            low += 1
            mid += 1
        elif arr[mid] == pivot:
            mid += 1
        else:
            arr[high], arr[mid] = arr[mid], arr[high]
            high -= 1

    return arr

# Example usage
arr = [2, 0, 2, 1, 1, 0]
sorted_arr = dutch_national_flag_sort(arr)
print("Sorted array:", sorted_arr)
```

Exchange Sort

Exchange Sort compares pairs of elements and swaps them if they are in the wrong order. This process is repeated until the entire array is sorted. The algorithm is conceptually similar to Bubble Sort but focuses solely on swapping elements to achieve sorting.

```python
def exchange_sort(arr):
    n = len(arr)
    for i in range(n):
        for j in range(i + 1, n):
            if arr[i] > arr[j]:
                arr[i], arr[j] = arr[j], arr[i]
    return arr

# Example usage
arr = [64, 34, 25, 12, 22, 11, 90]
sorted_arr = exchange_sort(arr)
print("Sorted array:", sorted_arr)
```

Gnome Sort

Gnome Sort is a simple comparison-based sorting algorithm that is similar to Insertion Sort but with a different approach to element positioning. It is also known as **Stupid Sort** or **Short Sort** due to its simplicity and inefficiency.

```python
def gnome_sort(arr):
    index = 0
    while index < len(arr):
        if index == 0 or arr[index] >= arr[index - 1]:
            index += 1
        else:
            arr[index], arr[index - 1] = arr[index - 1], arr[index]
            index -= 1
    return arr

# Example usage
arr = [34, 2, 10, -9, 6]
sorted_arr = gnome_sort(arr)
print("Sorted array:", sorted_arr)
```

Insertion Sort

Insertion Sort is a simple and intuitive comparison-based sorting algorithm. It builds the final sorted array one item at a time, making it similar to the way you might sort playing cards in your hands.

```python
def insertion_sort(arr):
    for i in range(1, len(arr)):
        key = arr[i]
        j = i - 1
        # Move elements of arr[0..i-1], that are greater than key, to one position ahead of their current position
        while j >= 0 and arr[j] > key:
            arr[j + 1] = arr[j]
            j -= 1
        arr[j + 1] = key
    return arr

# Example usage
arr = [64, 34, 25, 12, 22, 11, 90]
sorted_arr = insertion_sort(arr)
print("Sorted array:", sorted_arr)
```

Msd Radix Sort

Most Significant Digit (MSD) Radix Sort is a non-comparative sorting algorithm that processes numbers by their most significant digit first. It is particularly effective for sorting integers and strings and is often used when the range of possible values (digits) is limited.

```python
def get_digit(number, base, digit_index):
    return (number // base**digit_index) % base

def msd_radix_sort(arr, base=10, digit_index=0):
    if len(arr) <= 1 or digit_index >= len(str(max(arr))):
        return arr

    # Create buckets for each digit value
    buckets = [[] for _ in range(base)]

    # Place elements in the appropriate bucket
    for number in arr:
        digit = get_digit(number, base, digit_index)
        buckets[digit].append(number)

    # Sort each bucket recursively
    sorted_arr = []
    for bucket in buckets:
        sorted_bucket = msd_radix_sort(bucket, base, digit_index + 1)
        sorted_arr.extend(sorted_bucket)

    return sorted_arr

# Example usage
arr = [170, 45, 75, 90, 802, 24, 2, 66]
sorted_arr = msd_radix_sort(arr)
print("Sorted array:", sorted_arr)
```

Natural Sort

Natural Sort is a sorting algorithm designed to handle strings that contain both numbers and letters in a way that is more intuitive for human reading. For example, it sorts strings containing numeric values in a natural order, such as "file2" before "file10," which is often different from the lexicographic order used by standard sorting algorithms.

```python
import re

def natural_key(s):
    """
    Converts a string to a tuple that can be used for natural sorting.
    The tuple consists of alternating parts of digits and non-digits.
    """
    return [int(text) if text.isdigit() else text.lower() for text in re.split('([0-9]+)', s)]

def natural_sort(arr):
    """
    Sorts a list of strings using natural sorting.
    """
    return sorted(arr, key=natural_key)

# Example usage
arr = ["file1", "file10", "file2", "file20", "file11", "file21"]
sorted_arr = natural_sort(arr)
print("Sorted array:", sorted_arr)
```

Odd Even Sort

Odd-Even Sort is a simple parallel sorting algorithm that operates by repeatedly comparing and swapping adjacent elements in two phases: the odd phase and the even phase. It is a variation of the Bubble Sort algorithm designed to work well in parallel computing environments but is less efficient compared to more advanced sorting algorithms.

```python
def odd_even_sort(arr):
    n = len(arr)
    is_sorted = False
    while not is_sorted:
        is_sorted = True

        # Odd phase
        for i in range(1, n-1, 2):
            if arr[i] > arr[i+1]:
                arr[i], arr[i+1] = arr[i+1], arr[i]
                is_sorted = False

        # Even phase
        for i in range(0, n-1, 2):
            if arr[i] > arr[i+1]:
                arr[i], arr[i+1] = arr[i+1], arr[i]
                is_sorted = False

    return arr

# Example usage
arr = [64, 34, 25, 12, 22, 11, 90]
sorted_arr = odd_even_sort(arr)
print("Sorted array:", sorted_arr)
```

Quick Sort

Quick Sort is a widely used and efficient sorting algorithm based on the divide-and-conquer principle. It works by selecting a "pivot" element from the array and partitioning the other elements into two sub-arrays according to whether they are less than or greater than the pivot. This process is recursively applied to the sub-arrays.

```python
def quick_sort(arr):
    if len(arr) <= 1:
        return arr
    else:
        pivot = arr[len(arr) // 2]  # Choose the middle element as the pivot
        left = [x for x in arr if x < pivot]
        middle = [x for x in arr if x == pivot]
        right = [x for x in arr if x > pivot]
        return quick_sort(left) + middle + quick_sort(right)

# Example usage
arr = [3, 6, 1, 5, 4, 2]
sorted_arr = quick_sort(arr)
print("Sorted array:", sorted_arr)
```

Selection Sort

Selection Sort is a simple comparison-based sorting algorithm. It works by repeatedly selecting the smallest (or largest) element from the unsorted portion of the array and swapping it with the first element of the unsorted part.

```python
# Function to perform Selection Sort
def selection_sort(arr):
    n = len(arr)

    # Traverse through all array elements
    for i in range(n):
        # Find the minimum element in remaining unsorted array
        min_idx = i
        for j in range(i + 1, n):
            if arr[j] < arr[min_idx]:
                min_idx = j

        # Swap the found minimum element with the first element
        arr[i], arr[min_idx] = arr[min_idx], arr[i]

# Example usage
arr = [64, 25, 12, 22, 11]
selection_sort(arr)
print("Sorted array:", arr)
```

Shell Sort

Shell Sort is an optimization of Insertion Sort that allows the exchange of items that are far apart. It works by arranging the list of elements so that, starting with large gaps, elements far apart from each other can be compared and swapped. The gap size reduces gradually to 1, at which point the algorithm becomes a regular Insertion Sort.

```python
# Function to perform Shell Sort
def shell_sort(arr):
    n = len(arr)
    gap = n // 2  # Initialize the gap

    # Reduce the gap and sort elements that are gap distance apart
    while gap > 0:
        for i in range(gap, n):
            temp = arr[i]
            j = i

            # Shift elements that are gap distance apart
            while j >= gap and arr[j - gap] > temp:
                arr[j] = arr[j - gap]
                j -= gap

            arr[j] = temp

        gap //= 2  # Reduce the gap for the next iteration

# Example usage
arr = [12, 34, 54, 2, 3]
shell_sort(arr)
print("Sorted array:", arr)
```

Shrink Shell Sort

Shrink Shell Sort is a variation of the traditional Shell Sort, but with a slightly different approach to gap reduction. In standard Shell Sort, the gap is typically reduced by dividing the current gap by 2. In Shrink Shell Sort, the gap is reduced by a shrinking factor instead of halving. The shrinking factor is typically a constant greater than 1, like 1.3 or 2.

```python
# Function to perform Shrink Shell Sort
def shrink_shell_sort(arr, shrink_factor=1.3):
    n = len(arr)
    gap = int(n // shrink_factor)  # Initialize the gap

    while gap > 0:
        for i in range(gap, n):
            temp = arr[i]
            j = i

            # Perform the gap insertion sort
            while j >= gap and arr[j - gap] > temp:
                arr[j] = arr[j - gap]
                j -= gap

            arr[j] = temp

        gap = int(gap // shrink_factor)  # Reduce the gap by the shrinking factor

# Example usage
arr = [12, 34, 54, 2, 3]
shrink_shell_sort(arr)
print("Sorted array:", arr)
```

SlowSort

SlowSort is a highly inefficient and unusual sorting algorithm that is more of a theoretical curiosity than a practical algorithm. It belongs to the family of "divide and conquer" algorithms, but its time complexity is much worse than traditional sorts like Quick Sort or Merge Sort.

```python
# Function to perform SlowSort
def slow_sort(arr, i, j):
    if i >= j:
        return

    # Compute the midpoint
    mid = (i + j) // 2

    # Recursively sort the first half
    slow_sort(arr, i, mid)

    # Recursively sort the second half
    slow_sort(arr, mid + 1, j)

    # Compare and move the larger of the two
    if arr[mid] > arr[j]:
        arr[mid], arr[j] = arr[j], arr[mid]

    # Recursively sort the first half again
    slow_sort(arr, i, j - 1)

# Example usage
arr = [3, 1, 4, 1, 5, 9, 2, 6]
slow_sort(arr, 0, len(arr) - 1)
print("Sorted array:", arr)
```

Stooge Sort

Stooge Sort is another highly inefficient and theoretical sorting algorithm, similar to SlowSort, with very poor performance compared to practical algorithms like QuickSort or MergeSort. The algorithm works by recursively sorting portions of the array, with a peculiar approach of swapping elements from the ends of the list and then recursively applying the same process to different sections.

```python
# Function to perform Stooge Sort
def stooge_sort(arr, l, h):
    if l >= h:
        return

    # If the first element is larger than the last element, swap them
    if arr[l] > arr[h]:
        arr[l], arr[h] = arr[h], arr[l]

    # If there are at least three elements in the array
    if h - l + 1 > 2:
        t = (h - l + 1) // 3

        # Recursively sort the first two-thirds of the array
        stooge_sort(arr, l, h - t)

        # Recursively sort the last two-thirds of the array
        stooge_sort(arr, l + t, h)

        # Recursively sort the first two-thirds again
        stooge_sort(arr, l, h - t)

# Example usage
arr = [5, 3, 2, 4, 1]
stooge_sort(arr, 0, len(arr) - 1)
print("Sorted array:", arr)
```

Unknown Sort

Unknown Sort refers to a category of sorting algorithms where the exact details or implementation specifics of the algorithm are not well-defined or not widely known. This might be due to a few reasons, such as:

1. **Proprietary Algorithms**: The algorithm might be a proprietary or custom implementation that is not publicly documented.
2. **Experimental Algorithms**: It could be an experimental or academic algorithm that hasn't gained mainstream recognition or usage.
3. **Vague Terminology**: The term "Unknown Sort" might be used informally or generically to refer to sorting methods that are not standard or well-documented.

```python
def unknown_sort(arr):
    # Example: Using a simple known algorithm as a placeholder
    # Here, we use Bubble Sort as a placeholder
    n = len(arr)
    for i in range(n):
        for j in range(0, n-i-1):
            if arr[j] > arr[j+1]:
                arr[j], arr[j+1] = arr[j+1], arr[j]
    return arr

# Example usage
arr = [5, 21, 7, 23, 19, 10, 3, 11, 16, 20, 1, 9, 12, 4, 17, 18, 2, 8, 14, 6, 15, 13]
sorted_arr = unknown_sort(arr)
print("Sorted array:", sorted_arr)
```

Wiggle Sort

Wiggle Sort is a sorting algorithm that rearranges an array in a specific pattern. The goal is to sort the array such that the elements follow a "wiggle" pattern.

```python
def wiggle_sort(nums):
    # Iterate through the list
    for i in range(len(nums)):
        # For even index: nums[i] should be less than or equal to nums[i+1]
        if i % 2 == 0:
            if i + 1 < len(nums) and nums[i] > nums[i + 1]:
                nums[i], nums[i + 1] = nums[i + 1], nums[i]
        # For odd index: nums[i] should be greater than or equal to nums[i+1]
        else:
            if i + 1 < len(nums) and nums[i] < nums[i + 1]:
                nums[i], nums[i + 1] = nums[i + 1], nums[i]

# Example usage
arr = [3, 5, 2, 1, 6, 4]
wiggle_sort(arr)
print("Wiggle sorted array:", arr)
```

Searching Algorithms

Searching algorithms are techniques used to find specific elements or values within a data structure, such as an array or linked list. They are essential for data retrieval and are commonly used in various applications, including databases, file systems, and software development.

Binary Search

Binary Search is an efficient algorithm for finding a target value within a sorted array. It operates by repeatedly dividing the search interval in half, which makes it much faster than a linear search, especially for large datasets.

```python
def binary_search(arr, target):
    left, right = 0, len(arr) - 1

    while left <= right:
        mid = left + (right - left) // 2

        if arr[mid] == target:
            return mid  # Target found
        elif arr[mid] < target:
            left = mid + 1  # Search in the right half
        else:
            right = mid - 1  # Search in the left half

    return -1  # Target not found

# Example usage
arr = [1, 2, 3, 4, 5, 6, 7, 8, 9]
target = 5
result = binary_search(arr, target)

if result != -1:
    print(f"Target found at index {result}.")
else:
    print("Target not found.")
```

125

Double Linear Search

Double Linear Search is an algorithm that searches for a target value within a list by checking each element in a systematic way. The "double" aspect of this search refers to the fact that it may involve checking two lists or two different sequences simultaneously.

```python
def double_linear_search(list1, list2, target):
    # Check if both lists have the same length
    if len(list1) != len(list2):
        return "Both lists must have the same length."

    for i in range(len(list1)):
        # Check in the first list
        if list1[i] == target:
            return f"Found {target} in list1 at index {i}."
        # Check in the second list
        if list2[i] == target:
            return f"Found {target} in list2 at index {i}."

    return f"{target} not found in both lists."

# Example usage
list1 = [10, 20, 30, 40, 50]
list2 = [15, 25, 35, 45, 55]

target = 30
result = double_linear_search(list1, list2, target)
print(result)  # Output: Found 30 in list1 at index 2.

target = 25
result = double_linear_search(list1, list2, target)
print(result)  # Output: Found 25 in list2 at index 1.

target = 100
result = double_linear_search(list1, list2, target)
print(result)  # Output: 100 not found in both lists.
```

Hill Climbing

Hill Climbing is a heuristic search algorithm used for mathematical optimization problems. It belongs to the family of local search algorithms and is often applied in various domains, including artificial intelligence and machine learning, to find optimal solutions by incrementally improving an initial solution.

```python
import random

def objective_function(x):
    """Sample objective function: f(x) = -1 * (x - 3) ** 2 + 9 (a simple parabola)"""
    return -1 * (x - 3) ** 2 + 9

def hill_climbing(start, step_size=0.1, max_iterations=1000):
    current_solution = start
    current_value = objective_function(current_solution)

    for _ in range(max_iterations):
        # Generate neighboring solutions
        neighbors = [current_solution + step_size, current_solution - step_size]

        # Evaluate neighbors
        next_solution = max(neighbors, key=objective_function)
        next_value = objective_function(next_solution)

        # Check if the new solution is better
        if next_value > current_value:
            current_solution = next_solution
            current_value = next_value
        else:
            break  # Stop if no improvement

    return current_solution, current_value

# Example usage
```

```python
initial_solution = random.uniform(0, 6)   # Random initial guess
optimal_solution, optimal_value = hill_climbing(initial_solution)
print(f"Optimal Solution: {optimal_solution}, Optimal Value: {optimal_value}")
```

Interpolation Search

Interpolation Search is an algorithm for searching for a specific value in a sorted array. It improves on the binary search algorithm by estimating the position of the target value based on its value relative to the values at the boundaries of the array.

```python
def interpolation_search(arr, target):
    """Perform interpolation search on a sorted array."""
    low = 0
    high = len(arr) - 1

    while low <= high and target >= arr[low] and target <= arr[high]:
        # Estimate the position of the target
        pos = low + ((target - arr[low]) * (high - low) // (arr[high] - arr[low]))

        # Check if the target is found
        if arr[pos] == target:
            return pos
        # If the target is greater, ignore the left half
        elif arr[pos] < target:
            low = pos + 1
        # If the target is smaller, ignore the right half
        else:
            high = pos - 1

    return -1  # Target not found

# Example usage
sorted_array = [10, 20, 30, 40, 50, 60, 70, 80, 90, 100]
target_value = 70
result = interpolation_search(sorted_array, target_value)

if result != -1:
    print(f"Element found at index: {result}")
else:
    print("Element not found in the array.")
```

Jump Search

Jump Search is an algorithm used for searching for a specific value in a sorted array. It combines the advantages of linear search and binary search, making it more efficient than linear search while being simpler than binary search.

```python
import math

def jump_search(arr, target):
    """Perform jump search on a sorted array."""
    n = len(arr)
    jump = int(math.sqrt(n))  # Calculate block size
    prev = 0
    
    # Jump forward to find the block containing the target
    while prev < n and arr[min(jump, n) - 1] < target:
        prev = jump
        jump += int(math.sqrt(n))
        if prev >= n:
            return -1  # Target not found
    
    # Linear search within the identified block
    for i in range(prev, min(jump, n)):
        if arr[i] == target:
            return i  # Target found
    
    return -1  # Target not found

# Example usage
sorted_array = [1, 3, 5, 7, 9, 11, 13, 15, 17, 19]
target_value = 11
result = jump_search(sorted_array, target_value)

if result != -1:
    print(f"Element found at index: {result}")
else:
    print("Element not found in the array.")
```

Linear Search

Linear Search is the simplest searching algorithm used to find a specific value within a list or an array. It works by sequentially checking each element of the array until a match is found or the end of the list is reached. Linear Search can be applied to both sorted and unsorted arrays.

```python
def linear_search(arr, target):
    """Perform linear search on an array."""
    for index in range(len(arr)):
        if arr[index] == target:
            return index  # Target found
    return -1  # Target not found

# Example usage
array = [5, 3, 8, 4, 2]
target_value = 4
result = linear_search(array, target_value)

if result != -1:
    print(f"Element found at index: {result}")
else:
    print("Element not found in the array.")
```

Median of Medians

The **Median of Medians** is an algorithm used to find the **k-th smallest** (or largest) element in an unordered list efficiently. It provides a way to choose a good pivot for the Quickselect algorithm, improving its worst-case performance.

```python
def median_of_medians(arr):
    """Find the median of medians."""
    # Divide arr into groups of 5 and find medians
    n = len(arr)
    if n <= 5:
        return sorted(arr)[n // 2]  # Return median if 5 or fewer elements

    medians = []
    for i in range(0, n, 5):
        group = arr[i:i + 5]
        medians.append(sorted(group)[len(group) // 2])  # Find median of each group

    return median_of_medians(medians)  # Recursively find the median of medians

def partition(arr, pivot):
    """Partition the array around the pivot."""
    left = [x for x in arr if x < pivot]
    right = [x for x in arr if x > pivot]
    return left, right

def select_kth(arr, k):
    """Select the k-th smallest element using the Median of Medians."""
    if not 1 <= k <= len(arr):
        raise ValueError("k is out of bounds.")

    pivot = median_of_medians(arr)  # Find the median of medians
    left, right = partition(arr, pivot)
```

132

```python
    # Determine the size of the left partition
    size_left = len(left)

    if k <= size_left:
        return select_kth(left, k)  # k-th smallest is in the left partition
    elif k == size_left + 1:
        return pivot  # The pivot is the k-th smallest
    else:
        return select_kth(right, k - size_left - 1)  # Adjust k and search in the right partition

# Example usage
array = [7, 10, 4, 3, 20, 15]
k = 3
kth_smallest = select_kth(array, k)
print(f"The {k}-th smallest element is: {kth_smallest}")
```

Quick Select

Quick Select is an efficient algorithm to find the k-th smallest (or largest) element in an unordered list. It is related to the QuickSort sorting algorithm and operates using a similar partitioning technique.

```python
import random

def partition(arr, low, high, pivot_index):
    pivot_value = arr[pivot_index]
    # Move pivot to the end
    arr[pivot_index], arr[high] = arr[high], arr[pivot_index]
    store_index = low

    for i in range(low, high):
        if arr[i] < pivot_value:
            arr[store_index], arr[i] = arr[i], arr[store_index]
            store_index += 1

    # Move pivot to its final place
    arr[store_index], arr[high] = arr[high], arr[store_index]
    return store_index

def quick_select(arr, low, high, k):
    if low == high:  # If the list contains only one element
        return arr[low]

    # Select a random pivot_index between low and high
    pivot_index = random.randint(low, high)
    pivot_index = partition(arr, low, high, pivot_index)

    # The pivot is in its final sorted position
    if k == pivot_index:
        return arr[k]
    elif k < pivot_index:
```

134

```python
        return quick_select(arr, low, pivot_index - 1, k)
    else:
        return quick_select(arr, pivot_index + 1, high, k)

def find_kth_smallest(arr, k):
    """Find the k-th smallest element in the array."""
    if k < 1 or k > len(arr):
        raise ValueError("k is out of bounds.")
    return quick_select(arr, 0, len(arr) - 1, k - 1)  # k-1 for 0-based index

# Example usage
array = [7, 10, 4, 3, 20, 15]
k = 3
kth_smallest = find_kth_smallest(array, k)
print(f"The {k}-th smallest element is: {kth_smallest}")
```

Sentinel Linear Search

Sentinel Linear Search is an optimized version of the standard linear search algorithm that uses a sentinel value to reduce the number of comparisons needed to find an element in an array. The idea is to eliminate the need for bounds checking on each iteration, which can slightly improve performance.

```python
def sentinel_linear_search(arr, target):
    # Store the original last element
    last = arr[-1]
    # Set the last element to the target
    arr[-1] = target
    
    index = 0
    
    # Search for the target
    while arr[index] != target:
        index += 1
    
    # Restore the last element
    arr[-1] = last
    
    # Check if the target was found within the original bounds
    if index < len(arr) - 1 or arr[-1] == target:
        return index  # Return the index of the target
    else:
        return -1  # Target not found

# Example usage
array = [3, 5, 2, 1, 4]
target = 1
result = sentinel_linear_search(array, target)

if result != -1:
    print(f"Element {target} found at index: {result}")
else:
    print(f"Element {target} not found in the array.")
```

Simulated Annealing

Simulated Annealing is a probabilistic optimization algorithm inspired by the annealing process in metallurgy, where materials are heated and then slowly cooled to remove defects and optimize the structure. This algorithm is particularly effective for finding approximate solutions to complex optimization problems where the search space is large.

```python
import math
import random

def objective_function(x):
    """Example objective function to minimize."""
    return x**2

def random_neighbor(x):
    """Generate a random neighbor by adding a small random value."""
    return x + random.uniform(-1, 1)

def simulated_annealing(initial_solution, initial_temperature, cooling_rate):
    current_solution = initial_solution
    current_energy = objective_function(current_solution)
    temperature = initial_temperature

    while temperature > 1e-10:  # Termination condition
        new_solution = random_neighbor(current_solution)
        new_energy = objective_function(new_solution)

        energy_change = new_energy - current_energy

        # If the new solution is better, accept it
        if energy_change < 0:
            current_solution = new_solution
            current_energy = new_energy
        else:
            # Accept the new solution with a certain probability
```

```python
            acceptance_probability = math.exp(-energy_change / temperature)
            if random.random() < acceptance_probability:
                current_solution = new_solution
                current_energy = new_energy

        # Cool down the temperature
        temperature *= cooling_rate

    return current_solution, current_energy

# Example usage
initial_solution = 10.0  # Starting point
initial_temperature = 1000.0
cooling_rate = 0.95

optimal_solution, optimal_energy = simulated_annealing(initial_solution, initial_temperature, cooling_rate)

print(f"Optimal Solution: {optimal_solution}, Optimal Energy: {optimal_energy}")
```

Tabu Search

Tabu Search is a metaheuristic optimization algorithm that enhances the performance of local search methods by maintaining a memory structure called a "tabu list." This list keeps track of previously visited solutions or moves to prevent the algorithm from cycling back to them, thus avoiding local minima. Tabu Search is widely used for solving complex combinatorial optimization problems, such as scheduling, routing, and assignment problems.

```python
import random

def objective_function(solution):
    """Example objective function to minimize."""
    return sum(x**2 for x in solution)  # Simple quadratic function

def generate_neighbor(solution):
    """Generate a neighbor by modifying one element randomly."""
    neighbor = solution[:]
    index = random.randint(0, len(solution) - 1)
    neighbor[index] += random.uniform(-1, 1)  # Slight change
    return neighbor

def tabu_search(initial_solution, max_iterations, tabu_tenure):
    current_solution = initial_solution
    best_solution = current_solution
    best_energy = objective_function(current_solution)

    tabu_list = []
    tabu_counter = {}

    for iteration in range(max_iterations):
        neighborhood = [generate_neighbor(current_solution) for _ in range(100)]
        neighborhood = [sol for sol in neighborhood if sol not in tabu_list]
```

```python
        # Evaluate neighborhood solutions
        best_neighbor = None
        best_neighbor_energy = float('inf')

        for neighbor in neighborhood:
            energy = objective_function(neighbor)
            if energy < best_neighbor_energy:
                best_neighbor = neighbor
                best_neighbor_energy = energy

        # Update current solution
        if best_neighbor is not None:
            current_solution = best_neighbor
            # Update tabu list
            tabu_list.append(best_neighbor)
            tabu_counter[tuple(best_neighbor)] = tabu_tenure

            # Remove elements from the tabu list that have expired
            tabu_list = [sol for sol in tabu_list if tuple(sol) not in tabu_counter or tabu_counter[tuple(sol)] > 0]
            for key in list(tabu_counter.keys()):
                tabu_counter[key] -= 1

        # Update the best solution found so far
        if best_neighbor_energy < best_energy:
            best_solution = best_neighbor
            best_energy = best_neighbor_energy

    return best_solution, best_energy

# Example usage
initial_solution = [random.uniform(-10, 10) for _ in range(5)]  # Random initial solution
max_iterations = 1000
tabu_tenure = 5
```

```python
optimal_solution, optimal_energy = tabu_search(initial_solution, max_iterations, tabu_tenure)

print(f"Optimal Solution: {optimal_solution}, Optimal Energy: {optimal_energy}")
```

Ternary Search

Ternary Search is a divide-and-conquer algorithm that efficiently searches for a target value in a sorted array or list. It divides the array into three parts (rather than two, as in binary search) and determines which part to continue searching based on the target's value. This method can be particularly useful when the data is uniformly distributed.

```python
def ternary_search(arr, l, r, x):
    if r >= l:
        # Calculate midpoints
        m1 = l + (r - l) // 3
        m2 = r - (r - l) // 3

        # Check if x is at m1
        if arr[m1] == x:
            return m1
        # Check if x is at m2
        if arr[m2] == x:
            return m2

        # Determine which segment to search next
        if x < arr[m1]:
            return ternary_search(arr, l, m1 - 1, x)  # Search in the left segment
        elif x > arr[m2]:
            return ternary_search(arr, m2 + 1, r, x)  # Search in the right segment
        else:
            return ternary_search(arr, m1 + 1, m2 - 1, x)  # Search in the middle segment

    return -1  # If the element is not found

# Example usage
arr = [1, 2, 3, 4, 5, 6, 7, 8, 9, 10]
target = 7
result = ternary_search(arr, 0, len(arr) - 1, target)
```

```python
if result != -1:
    print(f"Element found at index: {result}")
else:
    print("Element not found in array")
```

Dynamic Programming

Dynamic programming (DP) is a powerful optimization technique used in algorithm design to solve complex problems by breaking them down into simpler subproblems. It is particularly useful for problems that exhibit overlapping subproblems and optimal substructure properties.

Catalan Numbers

Catalan numbers are a sequence of natural numbers that have many applications in combinatorial mathematics. They can be defined recursively and have various combinatorial interpretations, including counting the number of correct ways to arrange parentheses, the number of rooted binary trees, and more.

```python
def catalan_numbers(n):
    catalan = [0] * (n + 1)
    catalan[0] = 1   # C_0 = 1
    for i in range(1, n + 1):
        for j in range(i):
            catalan[i] += catalan[j] * catalan[i - 1 - j]
    return catalan

# Generate the first 10 Catalan numbers
print(catalan_numbers(10))
```

Climbing Stairs

The Climbing Stairs problem is a classic dynamic programming problem that involves calculating the number of distinct ways to climb a staircase given certain constraints on how many steps you can take at a time.

```python
def climb_stairs(n):
    if n == 1:
        return 1
    elif n == 2:
        return 2

    dp = [0] * (n + 1)
    dp[1] = 1  # One way to climb 1 step
    dp[2] = 2  # Two ways to climb 2 steps

    for i in range(3, n + 1):
        dp[i] = dp[i - 1] + dp[i - 2]

    return dp[n]

# Example usage
print(climb_stairs(3))   # Output: 3
print(climb_stairs(4))   # Output: 5
```

Combination Sum Lv

The Combination Sum problem is a classic backtracking problem that involves finding all unique combinations of numbers that sum up to a target value. This problem is often encountered in algorithm design and is essential for understanding recursion and backtracking techniques.

```python
def combination_sum(candidates, target):
    def backtrack(start, path, target):
        # Base case: if the target is met
        if target == 0:
            result.append(path)
            return
        # Explore the candidates
        for i in range(start, len(candidates)):
            if candidates[i] > target:  # Early stopping if the candidate exceeds the target
                continue
            # Include the candidate and continue searching
            backtrack(i, path + [candidates[i]], target - candidates[i])

    result = []
    candidates.sort()  # Optional: sorting can help with early stopping
    backtrack(0, [], target)
    return result

# Example usage
print(combination_sum([2, 3, 6, 7], 7))
# Output: [[2, 2, 3], [7]]
print(combination_sum([2, 3, 5], 8))
# Output: [[2, 2, 2, 2], [2, 3, 3], [3, 5]]
```

Edit Distance

The Edit Distance problem, also known as Levenshtein distance, is a classic dynamic programming problem that measures the minimum number of operations required to transform one string into another.

```python
def min_distance(word1, word2):
    m, n = len(word1), len(word2)

    # Create a DP table
    dp = [[0] * (n + 1) for _ in range(m + 1)]

    # Initialize the DP table
    for i in range(m + 1):
        dp[i][0] = i  # Deleting all characters from word1
    for j in range(n + 1):
        dp[0][j] = j  # Inserting all characters to word1 to get word2

    # Fill the DP table
    for i in range(1, m + 1):
        for j in range(1, n + 1):
            if word1[i - 1] == word2[j - 1]:  # Characters match
                dp[i][j] = dp[i - 1][j - 1]
            else:  # Characters do not match
                dp[i][j] = min(dp[i - 1][j] + 1,  # Deletion
                               dp[i][j - 1] + 1,  # Insertion
                               dp[i - 1][j - 1] + 1)  # Substitution

    return dp[m][n]

# Example usage
print(min_distance("horse", "ros"))  # Output: 3
print(min_distance("intention", "execution"))  # Output: 5
```

Factorial

The factorial of a non-negative integer nnn is the product of all positive integers less than or equal to nnn. It is denoted by n!n!n! and is defined as follows:

```python
# Iterative approach
def factorial_iterative(n):
    result = 1
    for i in range(2, n + 1):
        result *= i
    return result

# Recursive approach
def factorial_recursive(n):
    if n == 0:
        return 1
    else:
        return n * factorial_recursive(n - 1)

# Example usage
print(factorial_iterative(5))   # Output: 120
print(factorial_recursive(5))   # Output: 120
```

Fast Fibonacci

While the naive recursive method for computing Fibonacci numbers is inefficient due to its exponential time complexity, several efficient algorithms exist to compute Fibonacci numbers in logarithmic time.

```python
def matrix_mult(A, B):
    """Multiply two matrices A and B."""
    return [[A[0][0] * B[0][0] + A[0][1] * B[1][0], A[0][0] * B[0][1] + A[0][1] * B[1][1]],
            [A[1][0] * B[0][0] + A[1][1] * B[1][0], A[1][0] * B[0][1] + A[1][1] * B[1][1]]]

def matrix_pow(M, p):
    """Raise the matrix M to the power of p using exponentiation by squaring."""
    result = [[1, 0], [0, 1]]  # Identity matrix
    while p:
        if p % 2 == 1:
            result = matrix_mult(result, M)
        M = matrix_mult(M, M)
        p //= 2
    return result

def fib(n):
    """Return the nth Fibonacci number."""
    if n == 0:
        return 0
    if n == 1:
        return 1
    M = [[1, 1], [1, 0]]
    result = matrix_pow(M, n - 1)
    return result[0][0]  # F(n) is located at the top left corner

# Example usage
print(fib(10))  # Output: 55
print(fib(50))  # Output: 12586269025
```

Fizz Buzz

Fizz Buzz is a simple coding problem often used in programming interviews to assess a candidate's understanding of basic programming concepts, like loops, conditionals, and modulus arithmetic.

```python
def fizz_buzz(n):
    for i in range(1, n + 1):
        if i % 3 == 0 and i % 5 == 0:
            print("FizzBuzz")
        elif i % 3 == 0:
            print("Fizz")
        elif i % 5 == 0:
            print("Buzz")
        else:
            print(i)

# Example usage
fizz_buzz(15)
```

Integer Partition

The Integer Partition problem asks how many ways you can break down a number nnn into smaller positive numbers.

```python
def integer_partition(n):
    dp = [0] * (n + 1)  # Initialize an array to store partition counts
    dp[0] = 1  # Base case: one way to partition 0

    for i in range(1, n + 1):  # For each number i
        for j in range(i, n + 1):  # Update partitions for all numbers ≥ i
            dp[j] += dp[j - i]

    return dp[n]

# Example
n = 4
print(integer_partition(n))  # Output: 5
```

Longest Common Substring

The **Longest Common Substring** problem is a classical problem in computer science, where the goal is to find the longest substring that is common to two or more strings. The substring must be contiguous in both strings.

```python
def longest_common_substring(s1, s2):
    m, n = len(s1), len(s2)
    # Initialize a table to store lengths of longest common suffixes
    dp = [[0] * (n + 1) for _ in range(m + 1)]
    max_len = 0  # Store length of the longest common substring
    end_index = 0  # Store the ending index of the substring in s1

    for i in range(1, m + 1):
        for j in range(1, n + 1):
            if s1[i - 1] == s2[j - 1]:
                dp[i][j] = dp[i - 1][j - 1] + 1
                if dp[i][j] > max_len:
                    max_len = dp[i][j]
                    end_index = i
            else:
                dp[i][j] = 0

    # The longest common substring is from s1[end_index - max_len: end_index]
    return s1[end_index - max_len: end_index], max_len

# Example usage
s1 = "ABABC"
s2 = "BABC"
substring, length = longest_common_substring(s1, s2)
print(f"Longest Common Substring: '{substring}' with length {length}")
```

Palindrome Partitioning

The **Palindrome Partitioning** problem involves partitioning a string into the minimum number of substrings such that each substring is a palindrome.

```python
def is_palindrome(s, left, right):
    while left < right:
        if s[left] != s[right]:
            return False
        left += 1
        right -= 1
    return True

def partition(s):
    result = []
    current_partition = []

    def backtrack(start):
        if start >= len(s):
            result.append(current_partition[:])
            return
        for end in range(start, len(s)):
            if is_palindrome(s, start, end):
                current_partition.append(s[start:end + 1])
                backtrack(end + 1)
                current_partition.pop()

    backtrack(0)
    return result

# Example usage
s = "aab"
print(partition(s))
```

Tribonacci

The **Tribonacci sequence** is a variation of the Fibonacci sequence, where each term is the sum of the three preceding terms, instead of two. The sequence starts with the first three numbers as 0, 1, and 1, and each subsequent number is the sum of the previous three numbers.

```python
def tribonacci(n):
    if n == 0:
        return 0
    elif n == 1 or n == 2:
        return 1
    else:
        return tribonacci(n-1) + tribonacci(n-2) + tribonacci(n-3)

# Example usage
print(tribonacci(5))  # Output: 7
```

Word Break

The **Word Break** problem involves determining if a string can be segmented into a space-separated sequence of one or more dictionary words.

```python
def wordBreak(s, wordDict):
    n = len(s)
    # Create a DP array initialized to False
    dp = [False] * (n + 1)
    dp[0] = True  # Base case: empty string is always segmentable

    # Iterate over the length of the string
    for i in range(1, n + 1):
        for j in range(i):
            if dp[j] and s[j:i] in wordDict:
                dp[i] = True
                break

    return dp[n]

# Example usage
s = "leetcode"
wordDict = ["leet", "code"]
print(wordBreak(s, wordDict))  # Output: True
```

Coin Change

The **Coin Change** problem involves determining the minimum number of coins required to make a certain amount of money using given denominations. It can also involve counting the total number of combinations to achieve that amount.

```python
def coinChange(coins, amount):
    # Initialize the DP array
    dp = [float('inf')] * (amount + 1)
    dp[0] = 0  # Base case: no coins needed to make amount 0

    # Fill the DP array
    for coin in coins:
        for x in range(coin, amount + 1):
            dp[x] = min(dp[x], dp[x - coin] + 1)

    # If dp[amount] is still infinity, it means it's not possible to make that amount
    return dp[amount] if dp[amount] != float('inf') else -1

# Example usage
coins = [1, 2, 5]
amount = 11
print(coinChange(coins, amount))  # Output: 3
```

Ciphers

Ciphers are techniques used to encrypt and decrypt information, ensuring secure communication in the presence of adversaries. This section explores various cipher algorithms, their mathematical foundations, and their applications in cryptography.

Affine Cipher

The Affine cipher is a type of monoalphabetic substitution cipher where each letter in the plaintext is transformed using a linear function. This cipher combines the principles of modular arithmetic with a simple mathematical equation to encrypt and decrypt messages, making it both straightforward and intriguing.

```python
def gcd(a, b):
    while b:
        a, b = b, a % b
    return a

def mod_inverse(a, m):
    for x in range(1, m):
        if (a * x) % m == 1:
            return x
    return None

def affine_encrypt(plaintext, a, b):
    return ''.join(chr(((a * (ord(char) - 65) + b) % 26) + 65) for char in plaintext.upper() if char.isalpha())

def affine_decrypt(ciphertext, a, b):
    a_inv = mod_inverse(a, 26)
    if a_inv is None:
        return "Invalid 'a' value; must be coprime with 26."
    return ''.join(chr(((a_inv * ((ord(char) - 65) - b)) % 26) + 65) for char in ciphertext.upper() if char.isalpha())

# Example usage
plaintext = "HELLO"
a, b = 5, 8
ciphertext = affine_encrypt(plaintext, a, b)  # RCLLA

decrypted_text = affine_decrypt(ciphertext, a, b)  # HELLO

print(f"Ciphertext: {ciphertext}")  # Ciphertext: RCLLA
```

```python
print(f"Decrypted: {decrypted_text}")  # Decrypted: HELLO
```

Atbash

The Atbash cipher is a monoalphabetic substitution cipher that replaces each letter in the plaintext with its reverse counterpart in the alphabet. It is one of the simplest ciphers, and it is often used for fun or educational purposes.

```python
def atbash_cipher(text):
    # Create a mapping for Atbash
    alphabet = 'ABCDEFGHIJKLMNOPQRSTUVWXYZ'
    reversed_alphabet = alphabet[::-1]  # Reverse the alphabet

    # Create a translation table
    translation_table = str.maketrans(alphabet, reversed_alphabet)

    # Translate the text using the translation table
    return text.translate(translation_table)

# Example usage
plaintext = "HELLO"
ciphertext = atbash_cipher(plaintext)  # SVOLL
decrypted_text = atbash_cipher(ciphertext)  # HELLO

print(f"Ciphertext: {ciphertext}")  # Ciphertext: SVOLL
print(f"Decrypted: {decrypted_text}")  # Decrypted: HELLO
```

Base 16

Base 16, also known as the hexadecimal system, is a positional numeral system that uses 16 distinct symbols to represent values. The symbols used are the digits 0-9 and the letters A-F, where:

- **0-9** represent values zero to nine.
- **A** represents 10.
- **B** represents 11.
- **C** represents 12.
- **D** represents 13.
- **E** represents 14.
- **F** represents 15.

```python
def decimal_to_hexadecimal(n):
    if n < 0:
        return "Invalid input, please enter a non-negative integer."
    return hex(n).replace("0x", "").upper()  # Convert to hex and remove the '0x' prefix

def hexadecimal_to_decimal(hex_str):
    try:
        return int(hex_str, 16)  # Convert hex string to decimal
    except ValueError:
        return "Invalid hexadecimal input."

# Example usage
decimal_number = 419
hexadecimal_number = "1A3"

# Convert decimal to hexadecimal
hex_result = decimal_to_hexadecimal(decimal_number)  # Should return '1A3'
print(f"Decimal {decimal_number} to Hexadecimal: {hex_result}")
```

```python
# Convert hexadecimal to decimal
dec_result = hexadecimal_to_decimal(hexadecimal_number)  # Should return 419
print(f"Hexadecimal {hexadecimal_number} to Decimal: {dec_result}")
```

Beaufor Cipher

The Beaufort cipher is a polyalphabetic substitution cipher, similar to the Vigenère cipher, but it encrypts the plaintext using a keyword in a way that produces a more complex encryption. The Beaufort cipher uses a simple transformation method that can be easily understood.

```python
def beaufort_encrypt(plaintext, keyword):
    ciphertext = []
    keyword = keyword.upper()
    plaintext = plaintext.upper()
    
    keyword_repeated = (keyword * (len(plaintext) // len(keyword) + 1))[:len(plaintext)]
    
    for p, k in zip(plaintext, keyword_repeated):
        if p.isalpha():  # Ignore non-alpha characters
            p_index = ord(p) - ord('A')
            k_index = ord(k) - ord('A')
            c_index = (k_index - p_index + 26) % 26  # Beaufort formula
            ciphertext.append(chr(c_index + ord('A')))
        else:
            ciphertext.append(p)  # Keep non-alpha characters unchanged
    
    return ''.join(ciphertext)

def beaufort_decrypt(ciphertext, keyword):
    return beaufort_encrypt(ciphertext, keyword)  # Same process for decryption

# Example usage
plaintext = "HELLO"
keyword = "KEY"
ciphertext = beaufort_encrypt(plaintext, keyword)
decrypted_text = beaufort_decrypt(ciphertext, keyword)

print(f"Plaintext: {plaintext}")
```

```python
print(f"Ciphertext: {ciphertext}")
print(f"Decrypted Text: {decrypted_text}")
```

Caesar Cipher

The Caesar cipher is one of the simplest and most well-known encryption techniques. Named after Julius Caesar, who reportedly used it to communicate with his generals, the cipher works by shifting the letters of the alphabet by a fixed number of places.

```python
def caesar_encrypt(plaintext, shift):
    encrypted_text = []

    for char in plaintext:
        if char.isalpha():  # Check if character is a letter
            shift_base = ord('A') if char.isupper() else ord('a')
            encrypted_char = chr((ord(char) - shift_base + shift) % 26 + shift_base)
            encrypted_text.append(encrypted_char)
        else:
            encrypted_text.append(char)  # Non-alphabetical characters remain unchanged

    return ''.join(encrypted_text)

def caesar_decrypt(ciphertext, shift):
    decrypted_text = []

    for char in ciphertext:
        if char.isalpha():  # Check if character is a letter
            shift_base = ord('A') if char.isupper() else ord('a')
            decrypted_char = chr((ord(char) - shift_base - shift) % 26 + shift_base)
            decrypted_text.append(decrypted_char)
        else:
            decrypted_text.append(char)  # Non-alphabetical characters remain unchanged
```

```python
    return ''.join(decrypted_text)

# Example usage
shift = 3
plaintext = "HELLO, WORLD!"
ciphertext = caesar_encrypt(plaintext, shift)
print(f"Encrypted: {ciphertext}")

decrypted_text = caesar_decrypt(ciphertext, shift)
print(f"Decrypted: {decrypted_text}")
```

Morse Code

Morse Code is a method used to encode text characters into a series of dots (·) and dashes (−). Developed in the early 1830s and 1840s by Samuel Morse and Alfred Vail, it was originally used for long-distance communication over telegraph systems. Each letter of the alphabet and each numeral is represented by a unique sequence of dots and dashes, allowing for efficient transmission of information.

```python
# Morse Code Dictionary
morse_code_dict = {
    'A': '.-', 'B': '-...', 'C': '-.-.', 'D': '-..', 'E': '.',
    'F': '..-.', 'G': '--.', 'H': '....', 'I': '..', 'J': '.---',
    'K': '-.-', 'L': '.-..', 'M': '--', 'N': '-.', 'O': '---',
    'P': '.--.', 'Q': '--.-', 'R': '.-.', 'S': '...', 'T': '-',
    'U': '..-', 'V': '...-', 'W': '.--', 'X': '-..-', 'Y': '-.--',
    'Z': '--..', '1': '.----', '2': '..---', '3': '...--',
    '4': '....-', '5': '.....', '6': '-....', '7': '--...',
    '8': '---..', '9': '----.', '0': '-----'
}

def encode_morse(message):
    """Encode a message to Morse Code."""
    encoded_message = ' '.join(morse_code_dict.get(char.upper(), '') for char in message)
    return encoded_message

def decode_morse(morse_code):
    """Decode a Morse Code message."""
    reversed_dict = {value: key for key, value in morse_code_dict.items()}
```

```python
        decoded_message = ''.join(reversed_dict.get(code, '')
for code in morse_code.split(' '))
        return decoded_message

# Example Usage
if __name__ == "__main__":
    message = "HELLO WORLD"
    encoded = encode_morse(message)
    print(f"Encoded Morse Code: {encoded}")

    decoded = decode_morse(encoded.split(' '))
    print(f"Decoded Message: {decoded}")
```

Rot 13

ROT13 is a simple letter substitution cipher that replaces a letter with the 13th letter after it in the alphabet. It is a special case of the Caesar cipher, which is a type of substitution cipher where each letter in the plaintext is 'rotated' a certain number of places down the alphabet. Because the English alphabet has 26 letters, applying ROT13 twice will return the original text.

```python
def rot13(text):
    result = []

    for char in text:
        # Check if the character is uppercase
        if 'A' <= char <= 'Z':
            # Rotate within uppercase letters
            result.append(chr((ord(char) - ord('A') + 13) % 26 + ord('A')))
        # Check if the character is lowercase
        elif 'a' <= char <= 'z':
            # Rotate within lowercase letters
            result.append(chr((ord(char) - ord('a') + 13) % 26 + ord('a')))
        else:
            # Non-alphabetic characters remain unchanged
            result.append(char)

    return ''.join(result)

# Example usage
if __name__ == "__main__":
    plaintext = "HELLO WORLD"
    encrypted = rot13(plaintext)
    print("Encrypted:", encrypted)

    decrypted = rot13(encrypted)  # ROT13 applied again returns original
    print("Decrypted:", decrypted)
```

Rsa Cipher

The **RSA cipher** is a widely used public-key cryptographic system that allows secure data transmission. It was developed by Ron Rivest, Adi Shamir, and Leonard Adleman in 1977. RSA relies on the mathematical properties of large prime numbers and is widely used for secure data transmission, digital signatures, and key exchange.

```python
from sympy import mod_inverse

def generate_keys(p, q):
    n = p * q
    phi = (p - 1) * (q - 1)
    e = 65537  # Common choice for e
    d = mod_inverse(e, phi)
    return (n, e), (n, d)

def encrypt(public_key, plaintext):
    n, e = public_key
    ciphertext = pow(plaintext, e, n)
    return ciphertext

def decrypt(private_key, ciphertext):
    n, d = private_key
    plaintext = pow(ciphertext, d, n)
    return plaintext

# Example usage
if __name__ == "__main__":
    p = 61
    q = 53
    public_key, private_key = generate_keys(p, q)

    message = 123
    encrypted_message = encrypt(public_key, message)
    decrypted_message = decrypt(private_key, encrypted_message)

    print("Public Key:", public_key)
```

```python
print("Private Key:", private_key)
print("Original Message:", message)
print("Encrypted Message:", encrypted_message)
print("Decrypted Message:", decrypted_message)
```

Rsa Key Generator

RSA (Rivest–Shamir–Adleman) is one of the first public-key cryptosystems and is widely used for secure data transmission. The RSA algorithm relies on the difficulty of factoring the product of two large prime numbers.

```python
import random
from sympy import isprime, mod_inverse

def generate_prime_candidate(length):
    """Generate an odd prime number of specified bit length."""
    p = random.getrandbits(length)
    # Ensure p is odd
    p |= (1 << length - 1) | 1
    return p

def generate_prime_number(length):
    """Generate a prime number of specified bit length."""
    p = 4  # Initialize with a non-prime number
    while not isprime(p):
        p = generate_prime_candidate(length)
    return p

def generate_keys(bits):
    """Generate RSA keys."""
    # Generate two distinct prime numbers p and q
    p = generate_prime_number(bits)
    q = generate_prime_number(bits)

    # Ensure p and q are distinct
    while p == q:
        q = generate_prime_number(bits)

    # Calculate n and ϕ(n)
    n = p * q
    phi = (p - 1) * (q - 1)

    # Choose public exponent e
```

```python
    e = 65537  # Common choice for e
    
    # Calculate private exponent d
    d = mod_inverse(e, phi)
    
    # Public key (n, e) and Private key (n, d)
    public_key = (n, e)
    private_key = (n, d)
    
    return public_key, private_key

# Example usage
if __name__ == "__main__":
    bits = 512  # Bit length for p and q (use at least 2048 bits for security)
    public_key, private_key = generate_keys(bits)
    
    print("Public Key:", public_key)
    print("Private Key:", private_key)
```

Suffled Shift Cipher

The Shuffled Shift Cipher is a type of polyalphabetic substitution cipher that combines the concepts of shifting and shuffling to encrypt plaintext. It introduces randomness into the encryption process by shuffling the characters in the key after applying a shift, making it more secure than simpler ciphers.

```python
import random

def shuffle_key(key):
    """Shuffle the characters in the key."""
    key_list = list(key)
    random.shuffle(key_list)
    return ''.join(key_list)

def generate_key(plaintext, key):
    """Generate a key of the same length as the plaintext."""
    key = key.replace(" ", "").upper()  # Remove spaces and convert to uppercase
    if len(key) < len(plaintext):
        # Repeat the key if it's shorter than the plaintext
        key += (key * (len(plaintext) // len(key))) + key[:len(plaintext) % len(key)]
    return key[:len(plaintext)]

def encrypt(plaintext, key):
    """Encrypt the plaintext using the Shuffled Shift Cipher."""
    plaintext = plaintext.replace(" ", "").upper()  # Remove spaces and convert to uppercase
    key = generate_key(plaintext, key)
    ciphertext = ""

    for i in range(len(plaintext)):
        shifted_key = shuffle_key(key)
        c = (ord(plaintext[i]) - ord('A') + ord(shifted_key[i]) - ord('A')) % 26 + ord('A')
        ciphertext += chr(c)
```

```python
    return ciphertext

def decrypt(ciphertext, key):
    """Decrypt the ciphertext using the Shuffled Shift Cipher."""
    key = generate_key(ciphertext, key)
    plaintext = ""

    for i in range(len(ciphertext)):
        shifted_key = shuffle_key(key)
        p = (ord(ciphertext[i]) - ord('A') - (ord(shifted_key[i]) - ord('A')) + 26) % 26 + ord('A')
        plaintext += chr(p)

    return plaintext

# Example usage
if __name__ == "__main__":
    plaintext = "MEET AT DAWN"
    key = "SECRETKEY"

    encrypted = encrypt(plaintext, key)
    print("Encrypted:", encrypted)

    decrypted = decrypt(encrypted, key)
    print("Decrypted:", decrypted)
```

Maths

Mathematics is the foundation upon which algorithms are built. Understanding mathematical concepts is crucial for analyzing the efficiency, correctness, and complexity of algorithms.

Abs

The abs() function is used to return the absolute value of a number. The absolute value of a number is its distance from zero on the number line, without considering direction. This means that the result is always a non-negative number.

Syntax:

abs(x)

- **x**: A number (integer, float, or a complex number).

1. Using abs() with Integers

```
# Example with an integer
# The absolute value of -5 is 5
num = -5
absolute_value = abs(num)
print("The absolute value of", num, "is", absolute_value)
```

2. Using abs() with Floats

```
# Example with a float
num = -3.14
absolute_value = abs(num)
print("The absolute value of", num, "is", absolute_value)
# The absolute value of -3.14 is 3.14
```

3. Using `abs()` with Complex Numbers

- For complex numbers, `abs()` returns the magnitude of the complex number.

```python
# Example with a complex number
num = 3 + 4j
magnitude = abs(num)
print("The magnitude of the complex number", num, "is", magnitude)
# The magnitude of the complex number (3+4j) is 5.0
```

Addition without Arithmetic

You can perform addition without using arithmetic operators in Python by utilizing bitwise operations. The basic idea is to use the XOR operator to add numbers and the AND operator to determine where carries occur.

Bitwise Addition Explanation

- **XOR Operation (^):** This operation adds two bits and returns 1 if the bits are different, and 0 if they are the same. This gives us the sum without carrying.
- **AND Operation (&):** This operation finds the carry bits. If both bits are 1, it results in 1; otherwise, it results in 0.
- **Left Shift Operation (<<):** This operation shifts the carry bits one position to the left so that they can be added to the next higher bit position.

```python
def add_without_arithmetic(a, b):
    while b != 0:
        # Calculate carry
        carry = a & b

        # Sum without carrying
        a = a ^ b

        # Shift carry to the left
        b = carry << 1
```

```python
    return a

# Example usage
num1 = 5
num2 = 7
result = add_without_arithmetic(num1, num2)
print(f"The sum of {num1} and {num2} is {result}.")
```

Aliquot Sum

The **aliquot sum** of a number is the sum of its proper divisors, excluding the number itself. Proper divisors are the positive divisors of a number that do not include the number itself.

```python
def aliquot_sum(n):
    if n < 1:
        return 0  # Return 0 for non-positive numbers

    total = 0
    # Iterate through possible divisors
    for i in range(1, n // 2 + 1):
        if n % i == 0:  # Check if 'i' is a divisor
            total += i  # Add it to the total if it's a divisor

    return total


# Example usage
number = 12
result = aliquot_sum(number)
print(f"The aliquot sum of {number} is {result}.")
# The aliquot sum of 12 is 16.
```

Arc Length

The **arc length** of a curve is the distance along the curve between two points. In calculus, the arc length can be computed for a function defined by y=f(x)y = f(x)y=f(x) over a specific interval [a,b][a, b][a,b] using the following formula:

Where:

$$L = \int_a^b \sqrt{1 + \left(\frac{dy}{dx}\right)^2} \, dx$$

$\frac{dy}{dx}$ is the derivative of the function $f(x)$.

```python
import numpy as np
from scipy.integrate import quad

def arc_length(f, a, b):
    # Define the integrand for the arc length formula
    def integrand(x):
        return np.sqrt(1 + (np.gradient(f(x)))**2)
    
    # Numerical integration to calculate the arc length
    length, _ = quad(integrand, a, b)
    return length

# Example function: f(x) = x^2
def f(x):
    return x**2

# Calculate the arc length from x = 0 to x = 1
a = 0
b = 1
length = arc_length(f, a, b)

print(f"The arc length of the function from {a} to {b} is approximately {length:.4f}.")
```

Average Absolute Deviation

The **Average Absolute Deviation (AAD)** is a statistical measure that represents the average of the absolute deviations of each data point from the mean of the dataset. It provides insights into the dispersion of a set of values.

```python
import numpy as np

def average_absolute_deviation(data):
    # Calculate the mean
    mean = np.mean(data)
    # Calculate the absolute deviations
    absolute_deviations = np.abs(data - mean)
    # Calculate the Average Absolute Deviation
    aad = np.mean(absolute_deviations)
    return aad

# Example data
data = [10, 20, 30, 40, 50]

# Calculate the Average Absolute Deviation
aad = average_absolute_deviation(data)
print(f"Average Absolute Deviation: {aad:.2f}")
```

Average Mean

The **Average Mean**, commonly referred to simply as the **mean** or **average**, is a measure of central tendency that represents the sum of a set of values divided by the number of values in the dataset. It provides a way to summarize a dataset with a single value that represents the center of the data distribution.

```python
import numpy as np

def calculate_mean(data):
    # Calculate the mean using numpy
    mean = np.mean(data)
    return mean

# Example data
data = [10, 20, 30, 40, 50]

# Calculate the Mean
mean_value = calculate_mean(data)
print(f"Mean: {mean_value:.2f}")
```

Average Median

The **Average Median**, commonly referred to simply as the **median**, is another measure of central tendency. Unlike the mean, which can be heavily influenced by outliers, the median provides the middle value of a dataset when the numbers are arranged in order. It is a useful measure for understanding the center of a dataset, particularly when the data contains outliers or is skewed.

```python
import numpy as np

def calculate_median(data):
    # Calculate the median using numpy
    median = np.median(data)
    return median

# Example data
data = [10, 20, 30, 40, 50]

# Calculate the Median
median_value = calculate_median(data)
print(f"Median: {median_value:.2f}")
```

Average Mode

The **Average Mode**, commonly referred to simply as the **mode**, is a measure of central tendency that identifies the most frequently occurring value(s) in a dataset. Unlike the mean and median, which represent the center of the data in different ways, the mode gives insight into which value appears most often.

```python
from statistics import mode, multimode

def calculate_mode(data):
    try:
        # Calculate the mode using statistics module
        single_mode = mode(data)
        return single_mode
    except StatisticsError:
        return "No unique mode found"

def calculate_multimode(data):
    # Calculate the multimode
    modes = multimode(data)
    return modes

# Example data
data = [10, 20, 30, 20, 40, 50, 30]

# Calculate the Mode
mode_value = calculate_mode(data)
multimode_values = calculate_multimode(data)

print(f"Mode: {mode_value}")
print(f"All Modes: {multimode_values}")
```

Bailey Borwein Plouffe

The Bailey-Borwein-Plouffe (BBP) formula is an equation that allows for the computation of the nnn-th digit of π\piπ in base 161616 (hexadecimal) without needing to calculate the preceding digits. This property makes it particularly interesting and useful for various computational applications.

```python
def bbp_pi(n_terms):
    pi = 0
    for k in range(n_terms):
        pi += (1 / (16 ** k)) * (
            4 / (8 * k + 1) -
            2 / (8 * k + 4) -
            1 / (8 * k + 5) -
            1 / (8 * k + 6)
        )
    return pi

# Calculate pi using the BBP formula
n_terms = 100  # Number of terms to sum
pi_value = bbp_pi(n_terms)
print(f"Approximation of π using {n_terms} terms: {pi_value:.15f}")
```

Base Neg 2 Conversion

Base Negabinary (-2) Conversion is a method of representing numbers using base −2-2−2. Unlike traditional base conversions, the negabinary system allows for the representation of both positive and negative integers without the need for a separate sign bit.

```python
def decimal_to_negabinary(n):
    if n == 0:
        return "0"

    negabinary = []

    while n != 0:
        n, remainder = divmod(n, -2)
        if remainder < 0:
            remainder += 2
            n += 1
        negabinary.append(str(remainder))

    return ''.join(reversed(negabinary))

# Example Usage
number = 10
negabinary_representation = decimal_to_negabinary(number)
print(f"Decimal: {number} -> Negabinary: {negabinary_representation}")
```

Binary Exponentiation

The main idea behind Binary Exponentiation is to express the exponent in a binary format and use the properties of exponents to break down the computation.

```python
def binary_exponentiation(base, exponent):
    if exponent < 0:
        base = 1 / base
        exponent = -exponent
    result = 1
    while exponent > 0:
        # If exponent is odd, multiply the base with result
        if exponent % 2 == 1:
            result *= base
        # Square the base
        base *= base
        # Divide the exponent by 2
        exponent //= 2
    return result

# Example usage
base = 2
exponent = 10
print(f"{base}^{exponent} = {binary_exponentiation(base, exponent)}")
```

Binary Multiplication

Binary multiplication is the process of multiplying binary numbers, similar to the multiplication of decimal numbers but using base-2. This method involves shifting and adding, making it efficient for digital circuits and computer algorithms.

```python
def binary_multiplication(bin1, bin2):
    # Convert binary strings to integers
    num1 = int(bin1, 2)
    num2 = int(bin2, 2)

    # Perform multiplication
    product = num1 * num2

    # Convert the result back to binary
    return bin(product)[2:]  # Remove the '0b' prefix

# Example usage
bin1 = '1011'  # 11 in decimal
bin2 = '110'   # 6 in decimal
result = binary_multiplication(bin1, bin2)
print(f"{bin1} * {bin2} = {result}")
```

Binomial Coefficient

The Binomial Coefficient is a fundamental concept in combinatorics that represents the number of ways to choose kkk elements from a set of nnn elements, without regard to the order of selection.

Calculation Methods

1. **Using Factorials:** As defined above.
2. **Using Pascal's Triangle:** Construct Pascal's triangle up to nnn and read off the coefficient.
3. **Dynamic Programming:** A method to compute binomial coefficients without calculating factorials directly, which can be computationally expensive.

1. Using Factorials

```python
import math

def binomial_coefficient_factorial(n, k):
    if k < 0 or k > n:
        return 0
    return math.factorial(n) // (math.factorial(k) * math.factorial(n - k))

# Example usage
n = 5
k = 2
print(f"C({n}, {k}) = {binomial_coefficient_factorial(n, k)}")
```

2. Using Dynamic Programming

```python
def binomial_coefficient_dp(n, k):
    if k < 0 or k > n:
        return 0

    # Create a 2D array to store results of subproblems
    dp = [[0] * (k + 1) for _ in range(n + 1)]

    # Base cases
    for i in range(n + 1):
        dp[i][0] = 1  # C(n, 0) = 1
    for j in range(1, k + 1):
        dp[j][j] = 1  # C(n, n) = 1

    # Fill the dp table
    for i in range(1, n + 1):
        for j in range(1, min(i, k) + 1):
            dp[i][j] = dp[i - 1][j - 1] + dp[i - 1][j]

    return dp[n][k]

# Example usage
n = 5
k = 2
print(f"C({n}, {k}) = {binomial_coefficient_dp(n, k)}")
```

Binomial Distribution

The **Binomial Distribution** is a discrete probability distribution that describes the number of successes in a fixed number of independent Bernoulli trials (experiments with two possible outcomes: success or failure).

1. Calculating the Binomial Probability

```python
from math import comb

def binomial_probability(n, k, p):
    # Calculate the binomial probability
    return comb(n, k) * (p ** k) * ((1 - p) ** (n - k))

# Example usage
n = 10  # number of trials
k = 3   # number of successes
p = 0.5 # probability of success
probability = binomial_probability(n, k, p)
print(f"P(X = {k}) = {probability:.4f}")
```

2. Generating Random Variables from a Binomial Distribution

```python
import numpy as np
import matplotlib.pyplot as plt

n = 10  # number of trials
p = 0.5 # probability of success
size = 1000  # number of random variables to generate

# Generate random variables
random_variables = np.random.binomial(n, p, size)

# Plot the distribution
plt.hist(random_variables, bins=range(n + 2), density=True,
alpha=0.7, color='blue', edgecolor='black')
plt.title('Binomial Distribution (n=10, p=0.5)')
plt.xlabel('Number of Successes')
plt.ylabel('Probability')
plt.xticks(range(n + 1))
```

```
plt.grid()
plt.show()
```

Ceil

The **ceil** (short for "ceiling") function in mathematics is used to round a number up to the nearest integer. If the number is already an integer, it remains unchanged. In Python, you can use the math.ceil() function from the math module to achieve this.

```python
import math

# Examples of using math.ceil
numbers = [1.2, 2.5, -3.1, 4.0, 5.9]

# Applying ceil to each number
ceil_values = [math.ceil(num) for num in numbers]

# Displaying the results
for num, ceil_val in zip(numbers, ceil_values):
    print(f"Ceil of {num} is {ceil_val}")

# Ceil of 1.2 is 2
# Ceil of 2.5 is 3
# Ceil of -3.1 is -3
# Ceil of 4.0 is 4
# Ceil of 5.9 is 6
```

Chebyshev Distance

Chebyshev Distance, also known as the "maximum metric" or "L-infinity distance," is a measure of distance in a metric space that generalizes the notion of distance in a grid-based system. It is defined as the maximum absolute difference between the coordinates of two points.

```python
def chebyshev_distance(p, q):
    if len(p) != len(q):
        raise ValueError("Points must have the same dimension")
    return max(abs(pi - qi) for pi, qi in zip(p, q))

# Example usage
point_a = (1, 2, 3)
point_b = (4, 6, 1)

distance = chebyshev_distance(point_a, point_b)
print(f"Chebyshev Distance between {point_a} and {point_b} is: {distance}")

# Chebyshev Distance between (1, 2, 3) and (4, 6, 1) is: 4
```

Check Polygon

To **check if a point is inside a polygon**, one of the common algorithms used is the **Ray Casting Algorithm**. This algorithm counts how many times a ray starting from the point crosses the edges of the polygon. If the count is odd, the point is inside; if even, it's outside.

```python
def is_point_in_polygon(point, polygon):
    x, y = point
    n = len(polygon)
    inside = False

    p1x, p1y = polygon[0]
    for i in range(n + 1):
        p2x, p2y = polygon[i % n]
        if y > min(p1y, p2y):
            if y <= max(p1y, p2y):
                if x <= max(p1x, p2x):
                    if p1y != p2y:
                        xinters = (y - p1y) * (p2x - p1x) / (p2y - p1y) + p1x
                    if p1x == p2x or x <= xinters:
                        inside = not inside
        p1x, p1y = p2x, p2y

    return inside

# Example Usage
polygon = [(1, 1), (1, 3), (3, 3), (3, 1)]
point_inside = (2, 2)
point_outside = (4, 2)

print(f"Point {point_inside} is inside polygon: {is_point_in_polygon(point_inside, polygon)}")  # True
print(f"Point {point_outside} is inside polygon: {is_point_in_polygon(point_outside, polygon)}")  # False

# Point (2, 2) is inside polygon: True
# Point (4, 2) is inside polygon: False
```

Chudnovsky Algorithm

The **Chudnovsky algorithm** is an efficient method for calculating the digits of π (pi). It was developed by the Chudnovsky brothers in the 1980s and is particularly known for its rapid convergence, making it suitable for calculating millions of digits of π.

```python
from decimal import Decimal, getcontext

def chudnovsky_algorithm(precision):
    # Set the precision for Decimal calculations
    getcontext().prec = precision + 2  # Extra digits for accuracy
    
    C = 426880 * Decimal(10005).sqrt()
    K = 6
    M = 1
    L = 13591409
    S = L
    X = 1
    
    for k in range(1, precision):
        M = (K**3 - 16*K) * M // k**3   # Update M
        L += 545140134   # Update L
        X *= -262537412640768000   # Update X
        S += Decimal(M * L) / X   # Update S
        K += 12   # Increment K
    
    pi = C / S   # Calculate π
    return +pi   # Return π with the desired precision

# Example usage
precision = 100   # Number of decimal places
pi_value = chudnovsky_algorithm(precision)
print(f"Calculated value of π to {precision} decimal places:\n{pi_value}")
```

Collatz Sequence

The **Collatz sequence** (also known as the 3n + 1 problem) is a mathematical sequence defined as follows:

1. Start with any positive integer nnn.
2. If nnn is even, divide it by 2.
3. If nnn is odd, multiply it by 3 and add 1.
4. Repeat the process indefinitely.

The conjecture associated with the Collatz sequence is that no matter which positive integer you start with, you will eventually reach the number 1.

```python
def collatz_sequence(n):
    if n <= 0:
        raise ValueError("Input must be a positive integer.")

    sequence = [n]

    while n != 1:
        if n % 2 == 0:  # If n is even
            n //= 2
        else:  # If n is odd
            n = 3 * n + 1
        sequence.append(n)

    return sequence

# Example usage
start_number = 6
collatz_result = collatz_sequence(start_number)
print(f"Collatz sequence starting from {start_number}: {collatz_result}")
```

199

Combinations

Combinations are a way of selecting items from a larger pool where the order of selection does not matter.

```python
import math

def combinations(n, r):
    if r > n:
        return 0
    return math.factorial(n) // (math.factorial(r) * math.factorial(n - r))

# Example usage
n = 4
r = 2
result = combinations(n, r)
print(f"Number of combinations of choosing {r} from {n}: {result}")

# Number of combinations of choosing 2 from 4: 6
```

Continued Fraction

Continued Fractions are expressions obtained by iteratively breaking down fractions into their integer and fractional parts. They provide a way to represent real numbers through a sequence of integer terms and fractions. Continued fractions are particularly useful in number theory, approximation of real numbers, and for studying irrational numbers.

```python
def continued_fraction(p, q):
    if q == 0:
        raise ValueError("Denominator cannot be zero")

    result = []

    while q:
        a = p // q
        result.append(a)
        p, q = q, p - a * q

    return result

# Example usage
numerator = 22
denominator = 7
cf = continued_fraction(numerator, denominator)
print(f"The continued fraction of {numerator}/{denominator} is: {cf}")
```

Decimal Isolate

Decimal Isolation is a process used in programming and mathematics to separate the integer part of a decimal number from its fractional part. This can be useful in various applications, such as data processing, mathematical calculations, or formatting outputs.

```python
def decimal_isolate(number):
    # Get the integer part
    integer_part = int(number)
    # Get the fractional part
    fractional_part = number - integer_part
    return integer_part, fractional_part

# Example usage
number = 12.34
int_part, frac_part = decimal_isolate(number)
print(f"Integer Part: {int_part}, Fractional Part: {frac_part:.2f}")
```

Decimal to Fraction

Converting a decimal to a fraction involves expressing the decimal number as a ratio of two integers.

```python
from fractions import Fraction

def decimal_to_fraction(decimal_number):
    # Using the Fraction class to convert decimal to fraction
    fraction = Fraction(decimal_number).limit_denominator()
    return fraction

# Example usage
decimal_number = 0.75
result = decimal_to_fraction(decimal_number)
print(f"The fraction representation of {decimal_number} is {result}")
```

Double Factorial

The **double factorial** of a non-negative integer n, denoted as $n!!$, is the product of all integers from n down to 1 that have the same parity (even or odd) as n.

```python
def double_factorial(n):
    if n < 0:
        raise ValueError("Double factorial is not defined for negative integers.")
    if n == 0 or n == 1:
        return 1
    return n * double_factorial(n - 2)

# Example usage
print(double_factorial(6))  # Output: 48
print(double_factorial(7))  # Output: 105
print(double_factorial(0))  # Output: 1
```

Entropy

Entropy is a concept from information theory that quantifies the uncertainty or randomness in a system or dataset. In the context of data science and statistics, entropy is often used to measure the amount of information contained in a probability distribution. It can help in understanding the unpredictability of information content.

```python
import numpy as np

def calculate_entropy(probabilities):
    # Filter out zero probabilities
    probabilities = probabilities[probabilities > 0]
    return -np.sum(probabilities * np.log2(probabilities))

# Example usage
# Probabilities of outcomes
probabilities = np.array([0.5, 0.5])  # Fair coin
entropy_fair_coin = calculate_entropy(probabilities)

probabilities_biased = np.array([0.7, 0.3])  # Biased coin
entropy_biased_coin = calculate_entropy(probabilities_biased)

print(f"Entropy of fair coin: {entropy_fair_coin:.2f} bits")
# Output: 1.00 bits
print(f"Entropy of biased coin: {entropy_biased_coin:.2f} bits")
# Output: 0.88 bits
```

Euclidean Distance

Euclidean Distance is a measure of the straight-line distance between two points in Euclidean space. It's a widely used metric in various fields, including machine learning, statistics, and computer science, for comparing the similarity or dissimilarity between two data points.

```python
import numpy as np

def euclidean_distance(point1, point2):
    # Calculate the Euclidean distance between two points
    return np.sqrt(np.sum((np.array(point1) - np.array(point2)) ** 2))

# Example usage
point_a = (1, 2)
point_b = (4, 6)

distance = euclidean_distance(point_a, point_b)
print(f"Euclidean Distance between {point_a} and {point_b} is: {distance:.2f}")

# For a 3D example
point_c = (1, 2, 3)
point_d = (4, 6, 8)

distance_3d = euclidean_distance(point_c, point_d)
print(f"Euclidean Distance between {point_c} and {point_d} is: {distance_3d:.2f}")
```

Extended Euclidean Algorithm

The Extended Euclidean Algorithm is an extension of the Euclidean algorithm, which not only computes the greatest common divisor (GCD) of two integers aaa and bbb but also finds a way to express the GCD as a linear combination of aaa and bbb.

```python
def extended_gcd(a, b):
    if a == 0:
        return b, 0, 1  # Base case: gcd is b, x is 0, y is 1

    gcd, x1, y1 = extended_gcd(b % a, a)  # Recursive call

    # Update x and y using results of recursive call
    x = y1 - (b // a) * x1
    y = x1

    return gcd, x, y

# Example usage
a = 30
b = 21
gcd, x, y = extended_gcd(a, b)
print(f"The GCD of {a} and {b} is {gcd}, x = {x}, y = {y}")
```

Factors

Factors are integers that can be multiplied together to yield another integer. In other words, if aaa and bbb are integers and a×b=ca \times b = ca×b=c, then aaa and bbb are factors of ccc.

```python
def find_factors(n):
    factors = []
    for i in range(1, n + 1):
        if n % i == 0:  # Check if i is a factor of n
            factors.append(i)
    return factors

# Example usage
number = 12
factors_of_number = find_factors(number)
print(f"The factors of {number} are: {factors_of_number}")
```

Find Max

To find the maximum value in a collection of numbers, you can use various methods depending on the programming language or the context. Below are examples in Python to find the maximum value in a list, as well as explanations for different scenarios.

Example 1: Using Built-in Function

In Python, the easiest way to find the maximum value in a list is to use the built-in max() function.

```python
# Sample list of numbers
numbers = [3, 5, 1, 8, 2]

# Find the maximum value
max_value = max(numbers)

print(f"The maximum value is: {max_value}")
```

Example 2: Finding Maximum Manually

You can also find the maximum value manually by iterating through the list:

```python
# Sample list of numbers
numbers = [3, 5, 1, 8, 2]

# Initialize max_value to the first element
max_value = numbers[0]

# Iterate through the list to find the maximum value
for number in numbers:
    if number > max_value:
        max_value = number

print(f"The maximum value is: {max_value}")
```

Example 3: Using Recursion

If you want to find the maximum value using recursion, you can do it as follows:

```python
def find_max_recursive(lst):
    # Base case: if the list has only one element
    if len(lst) == 1:
        return lst[0]

    # Recursive case: compare the first element with the max of the rest
    return max(lst[0], find_max_recursive(lst[1:]))

# Sample list of numbers
numbers = [3, 5, 1, 8, 2]

# Find the maximum value recursively
max_value = find_max_recursive(numbers)

print(f"The maximum value is: {max_value}")
```

Example 4: Finding Maximum in a 2D List (Matrix)

If you have a 2D list (or matrix) and you want to find the maximum value, you can do it like this:

```python
# Sample 2D list (matrix)
matrix = [
    [3, 5, 1],
    [8, 2, 4],
    [6, 7, 9]
]

# Initialize max_value
max_value = matrix[0][0]

# Iterate through each row and column to find the maximum value
for row in matrix:
    for number in row:
        if number > max_value:
            max_value = number
```

```python
print(f"The maximum value in the matrix is: {max_value}")
```

Floor

The **floor** function is used to round a number down to the nearest integer. It effectively returns the largest integer less than or equal to a given number.

Example 1: Using `math.floor()`

Python provides a built-in module called math that includes the floor function.

```python
import math

# Sample numbers
numbers = [3.7, -2.1, 5.0, -3.8, 4.9]

# Applying floor function
floors = [math.floor(num) for num in numbers]

print(f"The floor values are: {floors}")
```

Example 2: Using Integer Division

You can also compute the floor of a positive number using integer division:

```python
# Sample numbers
numbers = [3.7, 2.9, 5.0]

# Finding floor values using integer division
floors = [int(num // 1) for num in numbers]

print(f"The floor values using integer division are: {floors}")
```

Example 3: Handling Negative Numbers

The `math.floor()` function correctly handles negative numbers by rounding down to the next lower integer.

```python
import math

# Sample negative numbers
negative_numbers = [-3.7, -2.1, -5.0]

# Applying floor function
floors = [math.floor(num) for num in negative_numbers]

print(f"The floor values for negative numbers are: {floors}")
```

Example 4: Using NumPy for Arrays

If you're working with arrays, the NumPy library provides a convenient way to apply the floor function to each element:

```python
import numpy as np

# Sample array
array = np.array([3.7, -2.1, 5.0, -3.8, 4.9])

# Applying floor function
floors = np.floor(array)

print(f"The floor values using NumPy are: {floors}")
```

Gamma

The **Gamma function** is a complex function that generalizes the factorial function to non-integer values.

Example 1: Using the `math` **module**

```python
import math

# Calculate Gamma for a positive integer
n = 5
gamma_n = math.gamma(n)   # Should return 24 (4!)
print(f"Gamma({n}) = {gamma_n}")

# Calculate Gamma for a non-integer
x = 2.5
gamma_x = math.gamma(x)   # Should return 1.329
print(f"Gamma({x}) = {gamma_x}")
```

Example 2: Using the scipy library
If you need more advanced features, the scipy library also provides the Gamma function:

```python
from scipy.special import gamma

# Calculate Gamma for a positive integer
n = 5
gamma_n = gamma(n)   # Should return 24.0 (4!)
print(f"Gamma({n}) = {gamma_n}")

# Calculate Gamma for a non-integer
x = 2.5
gamma_x = gamma(x)   # Should return 1.329
print(f"Gamma({x}) = {gamma_x}")
```

Digital Image Processing

Digital Image Processing (DIP) is a field that focuses on the manipulation and analysis of digital images using computer algorithms. It encompasses various techniques and processes that improve the quality of images or extract useful information from them. The goal of digital image processing is to convert an image into a form that is more suitable for analysis, interpretation, or storage.

Change Brightness

Changing the brightness of an image is one of the basic operations. Brightness can be increased or decreased by adjusting the intensity of the pixel values. In an 8-bit image, the pixel values typically range from 0 (black) to 255 (white). To change brightness, we either add or subtract a constant value to each pixel.

```python
import cv2
import numpy as np

# Function to change the brightness
def change_brightness(image, value):
    # Convert the image to the HSV color space
    hsv = cv2.cvtColor(image, cv2.COLOR_BGR2HSV)

    # Add the brightness value to the V channel
    h, s, v = cv2.split(hsv)
    v = np.clip(v + value, 0, 255)

    # Merge back the channels and convert to BGR
    final_hsv = cv2.merge((h, s, v))
    bright_image = cv2.cvtColor(final_hsv, cv2.COLOR_HSV2BGR)

    return bright_image

# Load an image from file
image = cv2.imread('input_image.jpg')

# Set brightness change value (positive for brighter, negative for darker)
brightness_value = 50

# Adjust brightness
bright_image = change_brightness(image, brightness_value)

# Save or display the brightened image
cv2.imwrite('brightened_image.jpg', bright_image)
cv2.imshow('Brightened Image', bright_image)
cv2.waitKey(0)
```

```
cv2.destroyAllWindows()
```

Change Contrast

To change the **contrast** of an image, you essentially adjust the difference between the light and dark areas of the image. A higher contrast will make dark areas darker and light areas lighter, while reducing contrast makes the image appear flatter or washed out.

```python
import cv2
import numpy as np

# Function to adjust contrast
def change_contrast(image, alpha, beta):
    # Apply the contrast and brightness formula
    contrast_image = cv2.convertScaleAbs(image, alpha=alpha, beta=beta)
    
    return contrast_image

# Load an image from file
image = cv2.imread('input_image.jpg')

# Set contrast value (alpha) and brightness (beta)
alpha = 1.5  # Contrast control (1.0-3.0)
beta = 0     # Brightness control (0-100)

# Adjust contrast
contrast_image = change_contrast(image, alpha, beta)

# Save or display the adjusted image
cv2.imwrite('contrast_image.jpg', contrast_image)
cv2.imshow('Contrast Adjusted Image', contrast_image)
cv2.waitKey(0)
cv2.destroyAllWindows()
```

Convert to Negative

Converting an image to its **negative** is a common image processing operation. In a negative image, each pixel's color is inverted, meaning dark areas become light and light areas become dark.

```python
import cv2

# Function to convert an image to its negative
def convert_to_negative(image):
    # Invert the image using 255 - pixel_value
    negative_image = 255 - image
    return negative_image

# Load an image from file
image = cv2.imread('input_image.jpg')

# Convert the image to negative
negative_image = convert_to_negative(image)

# Save or display the negative image
cv2.imwrite('negative_image.jpg', negative_image)
cv2.imshow('Negative Image', negative_image)
cv2.waitKey(0)
cv2.destroyAllWindows()
```

Burkes

Burkes dithering is an image processing technique used to convert a grayscale image into a binary image while preserving the image's visual details. It is a type of error diffusion dithering, a process that simulates continuous tones by distributing the quantization error to neighboring pixels, making the result more visually appealing, especially when reducing colors.

```python
import numpy as np
from PIL import Image

def burkes_dithering(image):
    # Convert image to grayscale if it's not already
    gray_image = image.convert('L')
    pixels = np.array(gray_image, dtype=np.float32)

    # Define the error diffusion matrix for Burkes
    error_matrix = np.array([[0, 0, 8/32, 4/32],
                             [2/32, 4/32, 8/32, 4/32, 2/32]])

    # Get image dimensions
    height, width = pixels.shape

    # Iterate through the pixels
    for y in range(height):
        for x in range(width):
            old_pixel = pixels[y, x]
            new_pixel = 255 if old_pixel > 127 else 0
            pixels[y, x] = new_pixel
            quant_error = old_pixel - new_pixel

            # Distribute the quantization error
            for j in range(error_matrix.shape[0]):
                for i in range(error_matrix.shape[1]):
                    if y + j < height and x + i - 2 < width and x + i - 2 >= 0:
                        pixels[y + j, x + i - 2] += quant_error * error_matrix[j, i]
```

```python
    # Convert back to uint8 format
    dithered_image = np.clip(pixels, 0,
255).astype(np.uint8)

    # Convert numpy array back to an image
    return Image.fromarray(dithered_image)

# Load image
image = Image.open('input_image.jpg')

# Apply Burkes dithering
dithered_image = burkes_dithering(image)

# Save or show the dithered image
dithered_image.save('burkes_dithered_image.jpg')
dithered_image.show()
```

Canny

Canny edge detection is a popular image processing algorithm used to detect edges in images. It was developed by John F. Canny in 1986 and is widely regarded as one of the best edge detection techniques. The algorithm aims to identify sharp changes in intensity (edges) in an image, which often correspond to object boundaries.

```python
import cv2
import numpy as np
from matplotlib import pyplot as plt

# Load the image
image = cv2.imread('input_image.jpg', cv2.IMREAD_GRAYSCALE)

# Apply GaussianBlur to reduce noise and smooth the image
blurred_image = cv2.GaussianBlur(image, (5, 5), 1.4)

# Apply Canny Edge Detection
edges = cv2.Canny(blurred_image, threshold1=100, threshold2=200)

# Display the results using matplotlib
plt.subplot(121), plt.imshow(image, cmap='gray')
plt.title('Original Image'), plt.xticks([]), plt.yticks([])

plt.subplot(122), plt.imshow(edges, cmap='gray')
plt.title('Canny Edge Detection'), plt.xticks([]), plt.yticks([])

plt.show()
```

Bilateral Filter

Bilateral filtering is an edge-preserving and noise-reducing smoothing filter used in image processing. It works by averaging pixels based on both their spatial proximity and their intensity differences. This makes it different from standard filters like Gaussian blur, which only consider spatial closeness. Bilateral filtering is particularly effective in reducing noise while maintaining sharp edges in an image.

```python
import cv2
import numpy as np
from matplotlib import pyplot as plt

# Load the image
image = cv2.imread('input_image.jpg')

# Apply Bilateral Filter
# Arguments: (source image, diameter of pixel neighborhood, sigmaColor, sigmaSpace)
filtered_image = cv2.bilateralFilter(image, d=15, sigmaColor=75, sigmaSpace=75)

# Display the original and filtered images
plt.subplot(121), plt.imshow(cv2.cvtColor(image, cv2.COLOR_BGR2RGB))
plt.title('Original Image'), plt.xticks([]), plt.yticks([])

plt.subplot(122), plt.imshow(cv2.cvtColor(filtered_image, cv2.COLOR_BGR2RGB))
plt.title('Bilateral Filtered Image'), plt.xticks([]), plt.yticks([])

plt.show()
```

Convolve

Convolution is a fundamental operation in image processing and computer vision. It involves applying a **kernel** (also called a filter or mask) to an image to produce a transformed image, typically for tasks like **blurring**, **sharpening**, **edge detection**, and **noise reduction**.

```python
import cv2
import numpy as np
from matplotlib import pyplot as plt

# Load the image
image = cv2.imread('input_image.jpg', cv2.IMREAD_GRAYSCALE)

# Define a kernel for convolution (3x3 example kernel)
# This is an edge detection kernel (Sobel kernel for horizontal edges)
kernel = np.array([[-1, -1, -1],
                   [ 0,  0,  0],
                   [ 1,  1,  1]])

# Apply the convolution using cv2.filter2D
convolved_image = cv2.filter2D(src=image, ddepth=-1, kernel=kernel)

# Display the original and convolved images
plt.subplot(121), plt.imshow(image, cmap='gray')
plt.title('Original Image'), plt.xticks([]), plt.yticks([])

plt.subplot(122), plt.imshow(convolved_image, cmap='gray')
plt.title('Convolved Image'), plt.xticks([]),
plt.yticks([])

plt.show()
```

Gabor Filter

A **Gabor filter** is a linear filter used in image processing and computer vision for texture analysis, edge detection, and feature extraction. It is particularly effective at capturing spatial frequencies and orientations in an image.

```python
import cv2
import numpy as np
from matplotlib import pyplot as plt

# Load the image
image = cv2.imread('input_image.jpg', cv2.IMREAD_GRAYSCALE)

# Define parameters for the Gabor filter
# You can experiment with different values for theta, lambda, etc.
ksize = 21  # Size of the filter
sigma = 5.0  # Standard deviation of the Gaussian
theta = np.pi / 4  # Orientation (45 degrees)
lamda = 10.0  # Wavelength of the sinusoidal factor
gamma = 0.5  # Aspect ratio
psi = 0  # Phase offset

# Create the Gabor filter
gabor_filter = cv2.getGaborKernel((ksize, ksize), sigma, theta, lamda, gamma, psi, ktype=cv2.CV_32F)

# Apply the Gabor filter to the image
filtered_image = cv2.filter2D(image, cv2.CV_8UC3, gabor_filter)

# Display the original and filtered images
plt.subplot(121), plt.imshow(image, cmap='gray')
plt.title('Original Image'), plt.xticks([]), plt.yticks([])

plt.subplot(122), plt.imshow(filtered_image, cmap='gray')
plt.title('Gabor Filtered Image'), plt.xticks([]), plt.yticks([])

plt.show()
```

Gaussian Filter

A **Gaussian filter** is a widely used filter in image processing for smoothing images and reducing noise. It works by averaging the pixels around a target pixel with weights that decrease with distance from the target pixel, following a Gaussian distribution. This results in a blurred image that retains the general structure while removing high-frequency noise

```python
import cv2
import numpy as np
from matplotlib import pyplot as plt

# Load the image
image = cv2.imread('input_image.jpg')

# Apply Gaussian Blur
# The second parameter (5, 5) is the kernel size; it should be positive and odd
# The third parameter is the standard deviation (0 means it is calculated from the kernel size)
blurred_image = cv2.GaussianBlur(image, (5, 5), 0)

# Display the original and blurred images
plt.subplot(121), plt.imshow(cv2.cvtColor(image, cv2.COLOR_BGR2RGB))
plt.title('Original Image'), plt.xticks([]), plt.yticks([])

plt.subplot(122), plt.imshow(cv2.cvtColor(blurred_image, cv2.COLOR_BGR2RGB))
plt.title('Gaussian Blurred Image'), plt.xticks([]), plt.yticks([])

plt.show()
```

Laplacian Filter

The **Laplacian filter** is an edge detection filter used in image processing to highlight areas of rapid intensity change, which typically correspond to edges. It calculates the second derivative of the image, emphasizing regions of the image where the intensity changes abruptly.

```python
import cv2
import numpy as np
from matplotlib import pyplot as plt

# Load the image
image = cv2.imread('input_image.jpg', cv2.IMREAD_GRAYSCALE)

# Apply Laplacian Filter
laplacian_image = cv2.Laplacian(image, cv2.CV_64F)

# Convert to absolute values to enhance visibility
laplacian_image = np.uint8(np.absolute(laplacian_image))

# Display the original and Laplacian images
plt.subplot(121), plt.imshow(image, cmap='gray')
plt.title('Original Image'), plt.xticks([]), plt.yticks([])

plt.subplot(122), plt.imshow(laplacian_image, cmap='gray')
plt.title('Laplacian Filtered Image'), plt.xticks([]), plt.yticks([])

plt.show()
```

Local Binary Pattern

Local Binary Pattern (LBP) is a texture descriptor used in computer vision and image processing. It is particularly effective for texture classification and analysis. The LBP operator summarizes the local structure of an image by converting each pixel into a binary number based on its neighborhood.

```python
import cv2
import numpy as np
import matplotlib.pyplot as plt

def local_binary_pattern(image, P=8, R=1):
    # Get image dimensions
    h, w = image.shape
    # Create an empty output image
    lbp_image = np.zeros((h, w), dtype=np.uint8)

    # Iterate through each pixel
    for i in range(R, h - R):
        for j in range(R, w - R):
            center = image[i, j]
            binary_string = ''

            # Compare center pixel with surrounding pixels
            for p in range(P):
                # Compute the angle for each pixel
                theta = 2 * np.pi * p / P
                x = int(i + R * np.sin(theta))
                y = int(j + R * np.cos(theta))
                # Append 1 or 0 to the binary string based on comparison
                binary_string += '1' if image[x, y] >= center else '0'

            # Convert binary string to decimal
            lbp_value = int(binary_string, 2)
            lbp_image[i, j] = lbp_value

    return lbp_image
```

```python
# Load the image in grayscale
image = cv2.imread('input_image.jpg', cv2.IMREAD_GRAYSCALE)

# Apply LBP
lbp_image = local_binary_pattern(image)

# Display the original and LBP images
plt.subplot(121), plt.imshow(image, cmap='gray')
plt.title('Original Image'), plt.xticks([]), plt.yticks([])

plt.subplot(122), plt.imshow(lbp_image, cmap='gray')
plt.title('LBP Image'), plt.xticks([]), plt.yticks([])

plt.show()
```

Median Filter

A **Median Filter** is a non-linear digital filtering technique commonly used in image processing to reduce noise while preserving edges. It works by replacing each pixel's value with the median value of the pixel's neighborhood. This makes it particularly effective for removing salt-and-pepper noise from images.

```python
import cv2
import numpy as np
import matplotlib.pyplot as plt

def median_filter(image, kernel_size=3):
    # Pad the image to handle edges
    pad_size = kernel_size // 2
    padded_image = cv2.copyMakeBorder(image, pad_size, pad_size, pad_size, pad_size, cv2.BORDER_REFLECT)
    # Create an output image
    filtered_image = np.zeros_like(image)
    
    # Get the dimensions of the image
    height, width = image.shape
    
    # Apply the median filter
    for i in range(height):
        for j in range(width):
            # Get the neighborhood of the current pixel
            neighborhood = padded_image[i:i + kernel_size, j:j + kernel_size].flatten()
            # Calculate the median
            median_value = np.median(neighborhood)
            # Assign the median value to the output image
            filtered_image[i, j] = median_value
    
    return filtered_image

# Load the image in grayscale
image = cv2.imread('input_image.jpg', cv2.IMREAD_GRAYSCALE)

# Apply the median filter
```

```python
filtered_image = median_filter(image, kernel_size=3)

# Display the original and filtered images
plt.subplot(121), plt.imshow(image, cmap='gray')
plt.title('Original Image'), plt.xticks([]), plt.yticks([])

plt.subplot(122), plt.imshow(filtered_image, cmap='gray')
plt.title('Median Filtered Image'), plt.xticks([]), plt.yticks([])

plt.show()
```

Sobel Filter

The **Sobel Filter** is a widely used edge detection technique in image processing. It is designed to compute the gradient of the image intensity at each pixel, emphasizing regions of high spatial frequency that correspond to edges. The Sobel operator combines Gaussian smoothing and differentiation, providing a good balance between noise reduction and edge detection.

```python
import cv2
import numpy as np
import matplotlib.pyplot as plt

def sobel_filter(image):
    # Define Sobel kernels
    sobel_x = np.array([[-1, 0, 1],
                        [-2, 0, 2],
                        [-1, 0, 1]])
    
    sobel_y = np.array([[1, 2, 1],
                        [0, 0, 0],
                        [-1, -2, -1]])
    
    # Apply Sobel filter
    gradient_x = cv2.filter2D(image, cv2.CV_64F, sobel_x)
    gradient_y = cv2.filter2D(image, cv2.CV_64F, sobel_y)
    
    # Calculate gradient magnitude
    gradient_magnitude = np.sqrt(gradient_x**2 + gradient_y**2)
    gradient_magnitude = np.uint8(np.clip(gradient_magnitude, 0, 255))  # Clip to 8-bit range
    
    return gradient_magnitude

# Load the image in grayscale
image = cv2.imread('input_image.jpg', cv2.IMREAD_GRAYSCALE)

# Apply the Sobel filter
sobel_image = sobel_filter(image)
```

```python
# Display the original and Sobel filtered images
plt.subplot(121), plt.imshow(image, cmap='gray')
plt.title('Original Image'), plt.xticks([]), plt.yticks([])

plt.subplot(122), plt.imshow(sobel_image, cmap='gray')
plt.title('Sobel Filtered Image'), plt.xticks([]),
plt.yticks([])

plt.show()
```

Histogram Stretch

Histogram Stretching (or histogram normalization) is a technique used in image processing to enhance the contrast of an image. This process involves spreading out the most frequent intensity values to cover the entire range of intensity levels, which often improves the overall visual quality of the image.

```python
import cv2
import numpy as np
import matplotlib.pyplot as plt

def histogram_stretch(image):
    # Get the minimum and maximum pixel values
    I_min = np.min(image)
    I_max = np.max(image)

    # Create a new image for the stretched output
    stretched_image = np.zeros(image.shape, dtype=np.uint8)

    # Apply histogram stretching formula
    stretched_image = ((image - I_min) * 255 / (I_max - I_min)).astype(np.uint8)

    return stretched_image

# Load the image in grayscale
image = cv2.imread('input_image.jpg', cv2.IMREAD_GRAYSCALE)

# Apply histogram stretching
stretched_image = histogram_stretch(image)

# Display the original and stretched images
plt.subplot(121), plt.imshow(image, cmap='gray')
plt.title('Original Image'), plt.xticks([]), plt.yticks([])

plt.subplot(122), plt.imshow(stretched_image, cmap='gray')
plt.title('Histogram Stretched Image'), plt.xticks([]), plt.yticks([])

plt.show()
```

Index Calculation

Index Calculation typically refers to a method used in various contexts such as data structures, image processing, and algorithms to determine the position of elements. Below are some common scenarios where index calculation is relevant, along with examples.

1. Array Index Calculation

In programming, when accessing elements in an array, you often need to calculate the index based on certain conditions. For example, if you have a 1D array and you want to access the nthn^{th}nth element, the index is simply n−1n-1n−1 (since indexing usually starts from 0).

```
arr = [10, 20, 30, 40, 50]
n = 3   # Let's say we want the 3rd element
index = n - 1
print("Element at index", index, "is", arr[index])
# Output: 30
```

2. Multi-Dimensional Array Index Calculation

In a 2D array (or matrix), the index calculation can be done using the formula:

- **Row Major Order:** `index = row * number_of_columns + column`
- **Column Major Order:** `index = column * number_of_rows + row`

```
matrix = [
    [1, 2, 3],
    [4, 5, 6],
    [7, 8, 9]
]
row = 1
col = 2
index = row * len(matrix[0]) + col  # len(matrix[0]) gives the number of columns
print("Element at index", index, "is", matrix[row][col])  # Output: 6
```

3. Image Processing Index Calculation

In image processing, images are often represented as 2D arrays of pixels. Accessing a pixel can involve calculating its index based on its coordinates.

```python
import numpy as np

# Create a 4x4 image (2D array)
image = np.array([
    [255, 0, 255, 0],
    [0, 255, 0, 255],
    [255, 255, 0, 0],
    [0, 0, 255, 255]
])

# Pixel coordinates (x, y)
x = 2   # Row index
y = 1   # Column index

# Access pixel value
pixel_value = image[x, y]
print("Pixel value at (", x, ",", y, ") is",
pixel_value)   # Output: 255
```

4. Hash Table Index Calculation

In hash tables, the index of a key is calculated using a hash function. The result is typically modulated by the size of the array to ensure it fits within the bounds.

```python
def hash_function(key, size):
    return hash(key) % size

size = 10   # Size of the hash table
key = "example"
index = hash_function(key, size)
print("Index for key", key, "is", index)
```

5. Index Calculation in Algorithms

In sorting or searching algorithms, index calculation can be critical to determining where to place or look for an element.

```python
def binary_search(arr, target):
    left, right = 0, len(arr) - 1
    while left <= right:
        mid = left + (right - left) // 2  # Prevent overflow
        if arr[mid] == target:
            return mid
        elif arr[mid] < target:
            left = mid + 1
        else:
            right = mid - 1
    return -1

arr = [1, 2, 3, 4, 5]
target = 3
index = binary_search(arr, target)
print("Index of target", target, "is", index)
# Output: 2
```

Dilation Operation

Dilation is a fundamental operation in image processing and mathematical morphology, used primarily for manipulating the shapes of objects in binary or grayscale images. It is often applied in the preprocessing and postprocessing stages of image analysis.

What is Dilation?
Dilation increases the size of the foreground objects (typically represented by white pixels in a binary image) in an image by adding pixels to the boundaries of those objects. This operation is particularly useful for filling small holes and gaps in the objects, connecting disjoint parts, and expanding the areas of interest.

```python
import cv2
import numpy as np
import matplotlib.pyplot as plt

# Create a binary image
image = np.array([[0, 0, 0, 0, 0],
                  [0, 1, 1, 0, 0],
                  [0, 1, 1, 1, 0],
                  [0, 0, 0, 0, 0]], dtype=np.uint8)

# Define the structuring element (3x3 square)
kernel = np.ones((3, 3), np.uint8)

# Apply dilation
dilated_image = cv2.dilate(image, kernel, iterations=1)

# Display the original and dilated images
plt.subplot(121), plt.imshow(image, cmap='gray')
plt.title('Original Image'), plt.xticks([]), plt.yticks([])

plt.subplot(122), plt.imshow(dilated_image, cmap='gray')
plt.title('Dilated Image'), plt.xticks([]), plt.yticks([])

plt.show()
```

Erosion Operation

Erosion is a fundamental operation in image processing and mathematical morphology, commonly used to process binary or grayscale images. It is often used to shrink the size of foreground objects (typically represented by white pixels) in an image.

What is Erosion?

Erosion reduces the boundaries of the foreground objects in an image. This operation is particularly useful for removing small-scale noise, separating connected objects, and refining the shape of objects by peeling away their outer layers.

```python
import cv2
import numpy as np
import matplotlib.pyplot as plt

# Create a binary image
image = np.array([[0, 0, 0, 0, 0],
                  [0, 1, 1, 0, 0],
                  [0, 1, 1, 1, 0],
                  [0, 0, 0, 0, 0]], dtype=np.uint8)

# Define the structuring element (3x3 square)
kernel = np.ones((3, 3), np.uint8)

# Apply erosion
eroded_image = cv2.erode(image, kernel, iterations=1)

# Display the original and eroded images
plt.subplot(121), plt.imshow(image, cmap='gray')
plt.title('Original Image'), plt.xticks([]), plt.yticks([])

plt.subplot(122), plt.imshow(eroded_image, cmap='gray')
plt.title('Eroded Image'), plt.xticks([]), plt.yticks([])

plt.show()
```

Resize

Resizing an image is a common operation in image processing that involves changing the dimensions of an image. This can be useful for various applications such as preparing images for web use, maintaining aspect ratios, or preparing datasets for machine learning.

```python
import cv2
import matplotlib.pyplot as plt

# Load an image
image = cv2.imread('path_to_your_image.jpg')

# Get original dimensions
original_height, original_width = image.shape[:2]

# Define new dimensions
new_width = 300
new_height = 200

# Resize the image
resized_image = cv2.resize(image, (new_width, new_height), interpolation=cv2.INTER_LINEAR)

# Display the original and resized images
plt.subplot(121), plt.imshow(cv2.cvtColor(image, cv2.COLOR_BGR2RGB))
plt.title('Original Image'), plt.xticks([]), plt.yticks([])

plt.subplot(122), plt.imshow(cv2.cvtColor(resized_image, cv2.COLOR_BGR2RGB))
plt.title('Resized Image'), plt.xticks([]), plt.yticks([])

plt.show()
```

Rotation

Rotating an image is another fundamental operation in digital image processing. It involves turning an image around a specified point (usually the center) by a certain angle. This operation can be useful for correcting the orientation of images, creating artistic effects, or preparing images for specific layouts.

```python
import cv2
import numpy as np
import matplotlib.pyplot as plt

# Load an image
image = cv2.imread('path_to_your_image.jpg')

# Get the dimensions of the image
(height, width) = image.shape[:2]

# Specify the angle of rotation
angle = 45  # degrees

# Get the rotation matrix
# The center of the image is defined as the point around which the image will be rotated
center = (width // 2, height // 2)
rotation_matrix = cv2.getRotationMatrix2D(center, angle, 1.0)  # 1.0 is the scale factor

# Perform the rotation
rotated_image = cv2.warpAffine(image, rotation_matrix, (width, height))

# Display the original and rotated images
plt.subplot(121), plt.imshow(cv2.cvtColor(image, cv2.COLOR_BGR2RGB))
plt.title('Original Image'), plt.xticks([]), plt.yticks([])

plt.subplot(122), plt.imshow(cv2.cvtColor(rotated_image, cv2.COLOR_BGR2RGB))
plt.title('Rotated Image'), plt.xticks([]), plt.yticks([])
```

```
plt.show()
```

Sepia

Applying a sepia tone to an image gives it a warm, brownish color that resembles photographs from the late 19th and early 20th centuries. This effect is often used in photography and image processing to create a vintage or nostalgic look.

How Sepia Works
The sepia effect is achieved by applying a specific color transformation to the RGB values of the image pixels. The transformation typically involves modifying the red, green, and blue color channels to create the characteristic warm brown tint.

```python
import cv2
import numpy as np
import matplotlib.pyplot as plt

# Load the image
image = cv2.imread('path_to_your_image.jpg')

# Define the sepia filter matrix
sepia_filter = np.array([[0.272, 0.534, 0.131],
                         [0.349, 0.686, 0.168],
                         [0.393, 0.769, 0.189]])

# Apply the sepia filter
sepia_image = cv2.transform(image, sepia_filter)

# Clip the values to be in the valid range [0, 255]
sepia_image = np.clip(sepia_image, 0, 255).astype(np.uint8)

# Display the original and sepia images
plt.subplot(121), plt.imshow(cv2.cvtColor(image,
cv2.COLOR_BGR2RGB))
plt.title('Original Image'), plt.xticks([]), plt.yticks([])

plt.subplot(122), plt.imshow(cv2.cvtColor(sepia_image,
cv2.COLOR_BGR2RGB))
plt.title('Sepia Image'), plt.xticks([]), plt.yticks([])

plt.show()
```

Strings

String algorithms are techniques used for processing, manipulating, and analyzing strings of text. These algorithms are crucial in various fields, including text processing, natural language processing, data compression, and bioinformatics.

Alternative String Arrange

1. Permutations

Generating all possible permutations of a string involves creating every possible arrangement of its characters.

```python
from itertools import permutations

def generate_permutations(s):
    return [''.join(p) for p in permutations(s)]

# Example usage
s = "abc"
permuts = generate_permutations(s)
print(f"Permutations of '{s}': {permuts}")
```

2. Combinations

Generating combinations involves selecting a subset of characters from a string and arranging them.

```python
from itertools import combinations

def generate_combinations(s, r):
    return [''.join(c) for c in combinations(s, r)]

# Example usage
s = "abc"
combs = generate_combinations(s, 2)
print(f"Combinations of '{s}' taken 2 at a time: {combs}")
```

3. String Rotation

Rotating a string involves moving characters from one end of the string to the other.

```python
def rotate_string(s, k):
    k = k % len(s)
    return s[k:] + s[:k]

# Example usage
s = "abcdef"
k = 2
rotated_s = rotate_string(s, k)
print(f"Rotated string: {rotated_s}")
```

4. Reversal

Reversing a string involves reversing the order of its characters.

```python
def reverse_string(s):
    return s[::-1]

# Example usage
s = "hello"
reversed_s = reverse_string(s)
print(f"Reversed string: {reversed_s}")
```

5. Alternating Characters

Rearranging a string such that characters alternate based on a given criterion (e.g., vowels and consonants).

```python
def alternate_chars(s):
    vowels = ''.join([c for c in s if c in 'aeiouAEIOU'])
    consonants = ''.join([c for c in s if c not in 'aeiouAEIOU'])
    result = []
    v, c = 0, 0
    for i in range(len(s)):
        if i % 2 == 0 and v < len(vowels):
            result.append(vowels[v])
            v += 1
        elif c < len(consonants):
            result.append(consonants[c])
            c += 1
    return ''.join(result)

# Example usage
s = "hello"
alternated_s = alternate_chars(s)
print(f"Alternated string: {alternated_s}")
```

6. Anagram Generation

Generating anagrams involves creating all possible rearrangements of a string's characters.

```python
from itertools import permutations

def generate_anagrams(s):
    return set(''.join(p) for p in permutations(s))

# Example usage
s = "abc"
anagrams = generate_anagrams(s)
print(f"Anagrams of '{s}': {anagrams}")
```

7. Lexicographic Permutation

Generating permutations in lexicographic order.

```python
from itertools import permutations

def lexicographic_permutations(s):
    return sorted(''.join(p) for p in permutations(s))

# Example usage
s = "abc"
lex_perms = lexicographic_permutations(s)
print(f"Lexicographic permutations of '{s}': {lex_perms}")
```

8. Rearranging to Form Largest Number

Rearranging digits of a number to form the largest possible number.

```python
def largest_number(s):
    return ''.join(sorted(s, reverse=True))

# Example usage
s = "3412"
largest = largest_number(s)
print(f"Largest number formed from '{s}': {largest}")
```

9. String Compression

Rearranging characters to compress the string (e.g., run-length encoding).

```python
def run_length_encoding(s):
    encoding = []
    i = 0
    while i < len(s):
        count = 1
        while i + 1 < len(s) and s[i] == s[i + 1]:
            i += 1
            count += 1
        encoding.append(s[i] + str(count))
        i += 1
    return ''.join(encoding)

# Example usage
s = "aaabbc"
compressed_s = run_length_encoding(s)
print(f"Compressed string: {compressed_s}")
```

Anagram

An anagram is a word or phrase formed by rearranging the letters of another word or phrase, using all the original letters exactly once. Anagramming is often used in puzzles and games, and it can also be useful in cryptography and data analysis.

1. Generating Anagrams

To generate all possible anagrams of a given string, you can use permutation algorithms to rearrange the characters.

Here's how you can do it in Python:

Using `itertools.permutations`

The `itertools.permutations` function generates all possible permutations of a string. To get unique anagrams, you can convert the results to a set.

```python
from itertools import permutations

def generate_anagrams(s):
    return set(''.join(p) for p in permutations(s))

# Example usage
s = "abc"
anagrams = generate_anagrams(s)
print(f"Anagrams of '{s}': {anagrams}")
```

2. Checking for Anagrams

To determine if two strings are anagrams of each other, you need to check if both strings contain the same characters with the same frequencies.

2.1. Using Sorting

Sorting both strings and comparing them is a straightforward method.

```python
def are_anagrams(s1, s2):
    return sorted(s1) == sorted(s2)

# Example usage
s1 = "listen"
s2 = "silent"
print(f"Are '{s1}' and '{s2}' anagrams? {are_anagrams(s1, s2)}")
```

2.2. Using Frequency Count

Counting the frequency of each character in both strings and comparing the counts.

```python
from collections import Counter

def are_anagrams(s1, s2):
    return Counter(s1) == Counter(s2)

# Example usage
s1 = "listen"
s2 = "silent"
print(f"Are '{s1}' and '{s2}' anagrams? {are_anagrams(s1, s2)}")
```

3. Generating Anagrams in Lexicographic Order

To generate anagrams in lexicographic order, you first generate all permutations and then sort them.

```python
from itertools import permutations

def lexicographic_anagrams(s):
    return sorted(''.join(p) for p in permutations(s))

# Example usage
s = "bca"
lex_anagrams = lexicographic_anagrams(s)
print(f"Lexicographic anagrams of '{s}': {lex_anagrams}")
```

Practical Applications
- **Puzzles and Games:** Anagrams are often used in word games and puzzles.
- **Cryptography:** Anagramming is used in cryptographic algorithms.
- **Text Analysis:** In data analysis, identifying anagrams can be useful for tasks like pattern recognition and text comparison.

Anagrams can be a fun and challenging way to work with strings, and understanding how to generate and check them efficiently can be useful in various applications.

Barcode Validator

A **Barcode Validator** is used to verify whether a given barcode (e.g., UPC, EAN) is valid by checking its structure and ensuring that it follows the correct format, usually by calculating and verifying a checksum.

```python
def validate_upc(upc_code):
    # Convert to string to handle it digit by digit
    upc_code = str(upc_code)
    
    if len(upc_code) != 12:
        return False  # UPC must be exactly 12 digits
    
    odd_sum = sum(int(upc_code[i]) for i in range(0, 11, 2))  # Sum of digits at odd positions
    even_sum = sum(int(upc_code[i]) for i in range(1, 11, 2))  # Sum of digits at even positions
    
    total = (odd_sum * 3) + even_sum
    check_digit = (10 - (total % 10)) % 10  # Calculate check digit
    
    return check_digit == int(upc_code[-1])  # Validate against last digit (check digit)

# Example Usage
upc_code = "036000291452"  # Valid UPC code
print(validate_upc(upc_code))  # Output: True
```

Bitap String Match

The **Bitap algorithm** (also known as the **Shift-Or algorithm**) is an approximate string matching algorithm used to search for substrings within a given text. It is particularly effective when working with patterns that allow for a small number of mismatches or "fuzzy" matches. The algorithm is based on **bitwise operations** and works efficiently for small patterns, especially when the alphabet size is small.

```python
def bitap_search(text, pattern):
    m = len(pattern)
    R = 0
    pattern_mask = {}

    # Initialize pattern mask table
    for i in range(m):
        pattern_mask[pattern[i]] = pattern_mask.get(pattern[i], 0) | (1 << i)

    current_state = 0

    for i in range(len(text)):
        if text[i] in pattern_mask:
            current_state = ((current_state << 1) | 1) & pattern_mask[text[i]]
        else:
            current_state = (current_state << 1) | 1

        if current_state & (1 << (m - 1)) == 0:
            return i - m + 1  # Pattern found at this position

    return -1  # Pattern not found

# Example usage
text = "hello world"
pattern = "world"
result = bitap_search(text, pattern)
print(f"Pattern found at index: {result}")
```

Camel Case to Snake Case

Converting a string from Camel Case to Snake Case can be done by identifying the uppercase letters and replacing them with an underscore followed by the lowercase version of the same letter.

```python
import re

def camel_to_snake(camel_str):
    # Use regex to identify uppercase letters and prepend with underscore
    snake_str = re.sub(r'(?<!^)(?=[A-Z])', '_', camel_str).lower()
    return snake_str

# Example usage
camel_case_string = "CamelCaseToSnakeCase"
snake_case_string = camel_to_snake(camel_case_string)
print(snake_case_string)
```

Capitalize

To capitalize a string in Python, you can use the `capitalize()` method, which converts the first character of the string to uppercase and makes all other characters lowercase.

```python
# Example usage of capitalize()
text = "hello world"
capitalized_text = text.capitalize()
print(capitalized_text)
```

Check Anagram

An **anagram** is when two strings can be rearranged to form each other. To check if two strings are anagrams, they must contain the same characters in the same frequencies.

```python
from collections import Counter

def are_anagrams(str1, str2):
    # Remove spaces and convert both strings to lowercase
    str1 = str1.replace(" ", "").lower()
    str2 = str2.replace(" ", "").lower()

    # Compare the frequency of characters in both strings
    return Counter(str1) == Counter(str2)

# Example usage
string1 = "listen"
string2 = "silent"
result = are_anagrams(string1, string2)
print(f"Are '{string1}' and '{string2}' anagrams? {result}")

string3 = "hello"
string4 = "world"
result2 = are_anagrams(string3, string4)
print(f"Are '{string3}' and '{string4}' anagrams? {result2}")
```

Count Vowels

To count the number of vowels in a string, you can iterate through the string and check each character to see if it's a vowel (either lowercase or uppercase). The vowels are: a, e, i, o, u.

```python
def count_vowels(s):
    # Define a set of vowels (both lowercase and uppercase)
    vowels = set("aeiouAEIOU")

    # Initialize a counter for vowels
    vowel_count = 0

    # Iterate over each character in the string
    for char in s:
        if char in vowels:
            vowel_count += 1

    return vowel_count

# Example usage
input_string = "Hello World"
vowel_count = count_vowels(input_string)
print(f"The number of vowels in '{input_string}' is: {vowel_count}")
```

Credit Card Validator

A **Credit Card Validator** typically checks whether a given credit card number is valid based on certain rules. One commonly used algorithm for this purpose is the **Luhn algorithm**.

```python
def luhn_check(card_number):
    # Convert the card number to a string to handle each digit
    card_number = str(card_number)
    
    # Reverse the card number and convert to integers for processing
    digits = [int(digit) for digit in card_number][::-1]
    
    # Double every second digit and subtract 9 if the result is greater than 9
    for i in range(1, len(digits), 2):
        digits[i] *= 2
        if digits[i] > 9:
            digits[i] -= 9
    
    # Sum all the digits
    total = sum(digits)
    
    # Check if total is divisible by 10
    return total % 10 == 0

# Example usage
card_numbers = [
    "4532015112830366",  # Valid Visa
    "6011514433546200",  # Valid Discover
    "4485680044297115",  # Valid Visa
    "1234567812345670",  # Invalid
]

for card in card_numbers:
    is_valid = luhn_check(card)
    print(f"Card Number: {card} - Valid: {is_valid}")
```

Detecting English Programmatically

Detecting whether a text is written in English can be accomplished through various methods, including statistical analysis, language models, and character frequency analysis.

```python
import nltk
from nltk.corpus import words

# Download the words corpus
nltk.download('words')

def is_english(text):
    # Get a set of English words
    english_words = set(words.words())
    
    # Preprocess the input text
    text = text.lower()  # Convert to lowercase
    words_in_text = text.split()  # Split the text into words
    
    # Count the number of words that are in the English word list
    count = sum(1 for word in words_in_text if word in english_words)
    
    # Calculate the percentage of words that are English
    percentage = count / len(words_in_text) if words_in_text else 0
    return percentage > 0.7  # Return True if more than 70% of the words are English

# Example usage
text1 = "This is a simple test."
text2 = "C'est une belle journée."

print(f"Text 1 is English: {is_english(text1)}")  # Output: True
print(f"Text 2 is English: {is_english(text2)}")  # Output: False
```

Is Srilankan Phone Number

To validate a Sri Lankan phone number, you can implement a function that checks for the correct format and rules governing Sri Lankan phone numbers.

```python
def is_valid_sri_lankan_phone_number(phone_number):
    # Check if the length of phone number is 10
    if len(phone_number) != 10:
        return False

    # Check if the phone number starts with '0' and is numeric
    if not (phone_number.startswith('0') and phone_number.isdigit()):
        return False

    # Check if the second digit is '7', '8', or '9'
    if phone_number[1] not in ['7', '8', '9']:
        return False

    return True

# Example usage
test_phone_numbers = [
    "0712345678",  # Valid mobile number
    "0812345678",  # Invalid mobile number (wrong second digit)
    "0912345678",  # Valid mobile number
    "12345678",    # Invalid (length)
    "0712345ABC"   # Invalid (non-numeric)
]

for number in test_phone_numbers:
    print(f"{number}: {'Valid Phone Number' if is_valid_sri_lankan_phone_number(number) else 'Invalid Phone Number'}")
```

Is Valid Email Address

To validate an email address, you can implement a function that checks if the email meets the standard format and rules. While many rules govern valid email formats, the most common validation uses a regular expression (regex) to ensure the structure conforms to the general syntax.

```python
import re

def is_valid_email(email):
    # Regular expression pattern for validating an email address
    pattern = r'^[a-zA-Z0-9._%+-]+@[a-zA-Z0-9.-]+\.[a-zA-Z]{2,}$'

    # Check if the email matches the pattern
    return re.match(pattern, email) is not None

# Example usage
test_emails = [
    "example@domain.com",    # Valid
    "user.name@domain.co",   # Valid
    "user-name@domain.com",  # Valid
    "user@domain",           # Invalid (no TLD)
    "user@.com",             # Invalid (invalid domain)
    "user@domain..com",      # Invalid (consecutive dots)
    "user@domain.c",         # Invalid (TLD too short)
    "user@domain.c1",        # Valid
]

for email in test_emails:
    print(f"{email}: {'Valid Email' if is_valid_email(email) else 'Invalid Email'}")
```

Join

1. Joining Strings

In Python, you can join elements of a list into a single string using the join() method.

```python
# List of strings
words = ["Hello", "world", "from", "ChatGPT"]

# Joining with a space
joined_string = " ".join(words)
print(joined_string)  # Output: "Hello world from ChatGPT"
```

2. Joining Lists of Strings with a Separator

You can use different separators when joining strings.

```python
# List of strings
fruits = ["apple", "banana", "cherry"]

# Joining with a comma
joined_fruits = ", ".join(fruits)
print(joined_fruits)  # Output: "apple, banana, cherry"
```

3. Joining Characters

You can also join characters in a string.

```python
# String to join characters with a hyphen
chars = "ABCDE"

# Joining characters with a hyphen
joined_chars = "-".join(chars)
print(joined_chars)  # Output: "A-B-C-D-E"
```

4. Joining Arrays in SQL

In databases, the term "join" often refers to combining rows from two or more tables based on a related column. For example, in SQL:

```sql
SELECT *
FROM employees
JOIN departments ON employees.department_id = departments.id;
```

Levenshtein Distance

The Levenshtein distance is a metric for measuring the difference between two strings. Specifically, it calculates the minimum number of single-character edits (insertions, deletions, or substitutions) required to change one string into the other. This concept is widely used in applications like spell checking, DNA sequencing, and natural language processing.

```python
def levenshtein_distance(s1, s2):
    # Create a matrix of zeros
    m, n = len(s1), len(s2)
    dp = [[0] * (n + 1) for _ in range(m + 1)]

    # Initialize the first row and column
    for i in range(m + 1):
        dp[i][0] = i  # Deleting all characters from s1
    for j in range(n + 1):
        dp[0][j] = j  # Inserting all characters into s1

    # Fill in the rest of the matrix
    for i in range(1, m + 1):
        for j in range(1, n + 1):
            if s1[i - 1] == s2[j - 1]:
                dp[i][j] = dp[i - 1][j - 1]  # No operation needed
            else:
                dp[i][j] = min(
                    dp[i - 1][j] + 1,      # Deletion
                    dp[i][j - 1] + 1,      # Insertion
                    dp[i - 1][j - 1] + 1   # Substitution
                )

    return dp[m][n]  # The distance is in the bottom-right cell

# Example usage
s1 = "kitten"
s2 = "sitting"
distance = levenshtein_distance(s1, s2)
```

```python
print(f"Levenshtein Distance between '{s1}' and '{s2}' is {distance}")
```

Lower

It seems like you're asking about a way to convert strings to lowercase in programming. In many programming languages, there are built-in functions or methods to handle this. Below, I'll provide examples in several popular programming languages.

In Python, you can use the lower() method to convert a string to lowercase.

```python
# Example
original_string = "Hello World!"
lowercase_string = original_string.lower()
print(lowercase_string)  # Output: "hello world!"
```

Naive String Search

The **Naive String Search** algorithm is a simple method for finding the occurrence of a pattern (substring) within a larger text (string). It works by checking for the pattern at every possible position in the text.

```python
def naive_string_search(text, pattern):
    n = len(text)
    m = len(pattern)
    indices = []

    # Iterate over each position in the text
    for i in range(n - m + 1):
        # Check if the pattern matches the substring of text
        match = True
        for j in range(m):
            if text[i + j] != pattern[j]:
                match = False
                break

        # If a match was found, store the index
        if match:
            indices.append(i)

    return indices

# Example usage
text = "abracadabra"
pattern = "abra"
matches = naive_string_search(text, pattern)
print(f"Pattern '{pattern}' found at indices: {matches}")
```

Ngram

An **N-gram** is a contiguous sequence of NNN items (words, characters, etc.) from a given sample of text or speech. N-grams are commonly used in natural language processing (NLP) and text mining to analyze and predict text patterns.

```python
def generate_ngrams(text, n):
    # Tokenize the text into words
    tokens = text.split()
    ngrams = []
    
    # Generate n-grams
    for i in range(len(tokens) - n + 1):
        ngram = tuple(tokens[i:i + n])  # Create a tuple of n tokens
        ngrams.append(ngram)
    
    return ngrams

# Example usage
text = "I love natural language processing"
n = 2  # Bigram
bigrams = generate_ngrams(text, n)
print(f"Bigrams: {bigrams}")
```

Pig Latin

Pig Latin is a playful language game often used in English-speaking countries.

```python
def pig_latin_converter(sentence):
    def convert_word(word):
        vowels = "aeiouAEIOU"
        if word[0] in vowels:
            # If the word starts with a vowel
            return word + "way"  # or "yay"
        else:
            # If the word starts with a consonant
            for index, letter in enumerate(word):
                if letter in vowels:
                    return word[index:] + word[:index] + "ay"
            return word + "ay"  # for words without vowels

    # Split the sentence into words, convert each, and join them back
    return ' '.join(convert_word(word) for word in sentence.split())

# Example usage
text = "I love programming in Python"
pig_latin_text = pig_latin_converter(text)
print(f"Pig Latin: {pig_latin_text}")
```

273

Prefix Function

The Prefix Function is a key concept used in string matching algorithms, especially in the Knuth-Morris-Pratt (KMP) algorithm. The prefix function for a string is an array where each element at index iii represents the length of the longest proper prefix of the substring s[0:i]s[0:i]s[0:i] which is also a suffix of this substring.

```python
def compute_prefix_function(s):
    n = len(s)
    pi = [0] * n  # Initialize prefix function array
    j = 0  # Length of the previous longest prefix

    # Start from the second character (index 1)
    for i in range(1, n):
        while j > 0 and s[i] != s[j]:
            j = pi[j - 1]  # Fallback to the previous prefix length

        if s[i] == s[j]:
            j += 1  # Match found, increase length of current prefix
        pi[i] = j  # Update the prefix function

    return pi

# Example usage
s = "abacab"
prefix_array = compute_prefix_function(s)
print(f"Prefix Function for '{s}': {prefix_array}")
```

Remove Duplicate

To remove duplicates from a list or string in Python, there are several approaches you can take depending on your requirements, such as maintaining the order of elements or not. Below, I'll cover a few methods for both lists and strings.

Removing Duplicates from a List

Using a Set (Unordered): This method removes duplicates but does not maintain the original order of the elements.

```python
def remove_duplicates_list(lst):
    return list(set(lst))

# Example usage
numbers = [1, 2, 2, 3, 4, 4, 5]
unique_numbers = remove_duplicates_list(numbers)
print(unique_numbers)  # Output: [1, 2, 3, 4, 5] (order may vary)
```

Using a Loop (Maintaining Order): This method maintains the original order of elements.

```python
def remove_duplicates_list_ordered(lst):
    unique_list = []
    for item in lst:
        if item not in unique_list:
            unique_list.append(item)
    return unique_list

# Example usage
numbers = [1, 2, 2, 3, 4, 4, 5]
unique_numbers = remove_duplicates_list_ordered(numbers)

print(unique_numbers)  # Output: [1, 2, 3, 4, 5]
```

Using Dictionary (Maintaining Order): In Python 3.7 and above, dictionaries maintain insertion order.

```python
def remove_duplicates_list_dict(lst):
    return list(dict.fromkeys(lst))

# Example usage
numbers = [1, 2, 2, 3, 4, 4, 5]
unique_numbers = remove_duplicates_list_dict(numbers)
print(unique_numbers)  # Output: [1, 2, 3, 4, 5]
```

Removing Duplicates from a String

Using a Set (Unordered): This method removes duplicates but does not maintain the original order of characters.

```python
def remove_duplicates_string(s):
    return ''.join(set(s))

# Example usage
text = "hello"
unique_text = remove_duplicates_string(text)
print(unique_text)  # Output: 'lohe' (order may vary)
```

Using a Loop (Maintaining Order): This method maintains the original order of characters.

```python
def remove_duplicates_string_ordered(s):
    unique_chars = []
    for char in s:
        if char not in unique_chars:
            unique_chars.append(char)
    return ''.join(unique_chars)

# Example usage
text = "hello"
unique_text = remove_duplicates_string_ordered(text)
print(unique_text)  # Output: 'helo'
```

Using Dictionary (Maintaining Order): This method uses the properties of dictionaries to maintain order.

```python
def remove_duplicates_string_dict(s):
    return ''.join(dict.fromkeys(s))

# Example usage
text = "hello"
unique_text = remove_duplicates_string_dict(text)
print(unique_text)  # Output: 'helo'
```

Reverse Letters

To reverse the letters in a string while maintaining the order of the words, you can use various methods in Python. Below are a few examples, including a simple function using slicing and another using a loop.

Method 1: Using Slicing

This is the most concise method to reverse the letters of a string.

```python
def reverse_letters(s):
    return ' '.join(word[::-1] for word in s.split())

# Example usage
text = "Hello World"
reversed_text = reverse_letters(text)
print(reversed_text)  # Output: "olleH dlroW"
```

Method 2: Using a Loop

This method uses a loop to reverse the letters of each word.

```python
def reverse_letters_loop(s):
    words = s.split()
    reversed_words = []
    for word in words:
        reversed_words.append(word[::-1])
    return ' '.join(reversed_words)

# Example usage
text = "Hello World"
reversed_text = reverse_letters_loop(text)

print(reversed_text)  # Output: "olleH dlroW"
```

Method 3: Using `reversed()` **Function**

You can also use the built-in `reversed()` function for a slightly different approach.

```python
def reverse_letters_reversed(s):
    words = s.split()
    reversed_words = [''.join(reversed(word)) for word in words]
    return ' '.join(reversed_words)

# Example usage
text = "Hello World"
reversed_text = reverse_letters_reversed(text)
print(reversed_text)  # Output: "olleH dlroW"
```

Reverse Words

To reverse the letters in a string while maintaining the order of the words, you can use various methods in Python. Below are a few examples, including a simple function using slicing and another using a loop.

Method 1: Using Slicing

This is the most concise method to reverse the letters of a string.

```python
def reverse_letters(s):
    return ' '.join(word[::-1] for word in s.split())

# Example usage
text = "Hello World"
reversed_text = reverse_letters(text)
print(reversed_text)  # Output: "olleH dlroW"
```

Method 2: Using a Loop

This method uses a loop to reverse the letters of each word.

```python
def reverse_letters_loop(s):
    words = s.split()
    reversed_words = []
    for word in words:
        reversed_words.append(word[::-1])
    return ' '.join(reversed_words)

# Example usage
text = "Hello World"
reversed_text = reverse_letters_loop(text)
print(reversed_text)  # Output: "olleH dlroW"
```

Method 3: Using reversed() Function

You can also use the built-in reversed() function for a slightly different approach.

```python
def reverse_letters_reversed(s):
    words = s.split()
    reversed_words = [''.join(reversed(word)) for word in words]
    return ' '.join(reversed_words)

# Example usage
text = "Hello World"
reversed_text = reverse_letters_reversed(text)
print(reversed_text)   # Output: "olleH dlroW"
```

Split

To split a string in Python, you can use the built-in `split()` method, which divides the string into a list of substrings based on a specified delimiter. By default, the `split()` method uses whitespace as the delimiter, but you can specify any character.

Basic Usage of `split()`

Default Split (whitespace): Splits the string at whitespace characters (spaces, tabs, newlines).

```python
text = "Hello World! Welcome to Python."
words = text.split()
print(words)   # Output: ['Hello', 'World!', 'Welcome', 'to', 'Python.']
```

Split by a Specific Character: You can specify a character to split the string. For example, splitting by a comma.

```python
text = "apple,banana,cherry"
fruits = text.split(',')
print(fruits)   # Output: ['apple', 'banana', 'cherry']
```

Limiting the Number of Splits: You can also limit the number of splits by passing a second argument to the `split()` method.

```python
text = "one two three four five"
limited_split = text.split(' ', 2)
print(limited_split)   # Output: ['one', 'two', 'three four five']
```

Examples of Using `split()`

Splitting a Sentence into Words:

```
sentence = "Python is great for data science."
words = sentence.split()
print(words)   # Output: ['Python', 'is', 'great', 'for', 'data', 'science.']
```

Splitting a CSV Line:

```
csv_line = "name,age,city"
fields = csv_line.split(',')
print(fields)  # Output: ['name', 'age', 'city']
```

Handling Multiple Delimiters: If you need to split using multiple delimiters, you can use the `re` module (regular expressions).

```
import re

text = "apple;banana,orange|grape"
fruits = re.split(r'[;,\|]', text)
print(fruits)  # Output: ['apple', 'banana', 'orange', 'grape']
```

Top K Frequent Words

To find the top K frequent words in a list of words, you can use a combination of Python's built-in data structures and libraries.

One common approach is to use the `collections.Counter` class to count the occurrences of each word and then retrieve the most common ones. Below is an implementation of this approach.

```python
from collections import Counter

def top_k_frequent_words(words, k):
    # Count the frequency of each word
    count = Counter(words)
    
    # Get the K most common words
    most_common = count.most_common(k)
    
    # Return only the words (not the counts)
    return [word for word, _ in most_common]

# Example usage
words = ["the", "day", "is", "sunny", "the", "the", "day", "is", "is"]
k = 2
top_words = top_k_frequent_words(words, k)

print("Top K Frequent Words:", top_words)
```

Wave String

If you're referring to creating a wave effect with a string, this usually means converting a string so that certain characters are capitalized in a wave-like pattern. This is often a fun way to visualize the "wave" concept, often used in programming challenges or string manipulation exercises.

```python
def wave_string(s):
    wave_list = []
    
    for i in range(len(s)):
        if s[i].isalpha():  # Only create a wave for alphabetic characters
            wave_list.append(s[:i] + s[i].upper() + s[i+1:])
    
    return wave_list

# Example usage
input_string = "hello"
wave_output = wave_string(input_string)

print("Wave Effect:")
for wave in wave_output:
    print(wave)
```

Word Patterns

Word patterns often involve checking if a string matches a specific pattern. For example, given a string like "abab" and a pattern "xyxy", we need to determine if the characters can be mapped consistently. In this example, 'x' could represent 'a' and 'y' could represent 'b'.

```python
def word_pattern(pattern: str, s: str) -> bool:
    words = s.split()
    if len(pattern) != len(words):
        return False

    char_to_word = {}
    word_to_char = {}

    for p, w in zip(pattern, words):
        if p not in char_to_word:
            char_to_word[p] = w
        if w not in word_to_char:
            word_to_char[w] = p

        # Check if the mapping is consistent
        if char_to_word[p] != w or word_to_char[w] != p:
            return False

    return True

# Example usage
pattern = "abba"
s = "dog cat cat dog"
match_result = word_pattern(pattern, s)

print(f"Does the string '{s}' match the pattern '{pattern}'? {match_result}")
```

Z Function

The **Z function** is a useful algorithm in string processing that helps in pattern matching and substring searching. For a given string, the Z function computes an array where the value at each position `i` represents the length of the longest substring starting from `i` that is also a prefix of the string.

```python
def z_function(s: str) -> list:
    n = len(s)
    Z = [0] * n
    L, R, K = 0, 0, 0

    for i in range(1, n):
        if i > R:
            L, R = i, i
            while R < n and s[R] == s[R - L]:
                R += 1
            Z[i] = R - L
            R -= 1
        else:
            K = i - L
            if Z[K] < R - i + 1:
                Z[i] = Z[K]
            else:
                L = i
                while R < n and s[R] == s[R - L]:
                    R += 1
                Z[i] = R - L
                R -= 1

    return Z

# Example usage
input_string = "aabcaabxaaaz"
z_array = z_function(input_string)

print("Z Array:", z_array)
```

Machine Learning

Machine Learning (ML) is a subset of artificial intelligence (AI) that focuses on the development of algorithms and statistical models enabling computers to perform specific tasks without explicit instructions. Instead, ML systems learn from data, identify patterns, and make decisions or predictions based on that information. It encompasses various techniques, including supervised learning, unsupervised learning, and reinforcement learning, each suited for different types of tasks and data.

Apriori Algorithm

The Apriori algorithm is a classic algorithm used in data mining for association rule learning. It identifies frequent itemsets in transactional data and derives association rules from these itemsets. This algorithm is particularly useful in market basket analysis, where it helps discover sets of products that frequently co-occur in transactions.

```python
from itertools import combinations
from collections import defaultdict

def apriori(transactions, min_support):
    item_count = defaultdict(int)
    freq_itemsets = []

    # Count support for single items
    for transaction in transactions:
        for item in transaction:
            item_count[item] += 1

    # Filter items based on min_support
    num_transactions = len(transactions)
    freq_items = {item for item, count in item_count.items() if count / num_transactions >= min_support}

    # Generate frequent itemsets
    k = 1
    while freq_items:
        freq_itemsets.append(freq_items)
        k += 1
        item_sets = combinations(freq_items, k)
        item_count = defaultdict(int)

        # Count support for candidate itemsets
        for transaction in transactions:
            for item_set in item_sets:
                if set(item_set).issubset(transaction):
                    item_count[item_set] += 1
```

```python
        # Filter candidate itemsets based on min_support
        freq_items = {item_set for item_set, count in item_count.items() if count / num_transactions >= min_support}

    return freq_itemsets

# Example usage
transactions = [
    ['milk', 'bread', 'diapers'],
    ['bread', 'butter'],
    ['milk', 'diapers', 'bread', 'butter'],
    ['milk', 'bread'],
    ['diapers', 'bread']
]
min_support = 0.4
frequent_itemsets = apriori(transactions, min_support)

# Output the frequent itemsets
print(frequent_itemsets)  # Output: [{('bread',)}, {('milk',)}, {('diapers',)}, {('bread', 'diapers')}, ...]
```

Automatic Differentiation

Automatic differentiation (AD) is a computational technique used to efficiently compute derivatives of functions expressed as computer programs. Unlike symbolic differentiation, which manipulates expressions algebraically, or numerical differentiation, which approximates derivatives using finite differences, automatic differentiation computes derivatives to machine precision using the chain rule of calculus.

```python
class DualNumber:
    def __init__(self, value, derivative):
        self.value = value
        self.derivative = derivative

    def __add__(self, other):
        return DualNumber(self.value + other.value, self.derivative + other.derivative)

    def __mul__(self, other):
        return DualNumber(self.value * other.value, self.value * other.derivative + self.derivative * other.value)

    def __repr__(self):
        return f"DualNumber(value={self.value}, derivative={self.derivative})"

def func(x):
    return x * x + x

def autodiff_func(x):
    x_dual = DualNumber(x, 1)  # Initialize with derivative 1
    return func(x_dual)

# Example usage
x = 2.0
result = autodiff_func(x)
```

```python
print(f"Function value: {result.value}, Derivative: {result.derivative}")  # Output: Function value: 6.0, Derivative: 5.0
```

Data Transformations

Data transformations involve the process of converting data from one format or structure into another to make it more suitable for analysis, modeling, or visualization. This can include normalization, aggregation, encoding, and reshaping data to facilitate better insights, reduce complexity, and enhance model performance.

```python
import pandas as pd
from sklearn.preprocessing import MinMaxScaler, OneHotEncoder

# Sample DataFrame
data = {
    'age': [25, 30, 35, 40, 45],
    'income': [50000, 60000, 70000, 80000, 90000],
    'city': ['New York', 'Los Angeles', 'Chicago', 'Houston', 'Phoenix']
}
df = pd.DataFrame(data)

# 1. Normalization (Min-Max Scaling)
scaler = MinMaxScaler()
df[['age', 'income']] = scaler.fit_transform(df[['age', 'income']])

# 2. One-Hot Encoding
df = pd.get_dummies(df, columns=['city'], drop_first=True)

# Output the transformed DataFrame
print(df)
```

Decision Tree

A Decision Tree is a popular machine learning algorithm used for classification and regression tasks. It works by recursively splitting the data into subsets based on the value of input features, leading to a tree-like model of decisions. Each internal node represents a feature (or attribute), each branch represents a decision rule, and each leaf node represents an outcome or class label.

```python
import pandas as pd
from sklearn.model_selection import train_test_split
from sklearn.tree import DecisionTreeClassifier, export_text

# Sample dataset
data = {
    'Feature1': [1, 2, 3, 4, 5, 6],
    'Feature2': ['A', 'A', 'B', 'B', 'A', 'B'],
    'Class': [0, 0, 1, 1, 0, 1]
}
df = pd.DataFrame(data)

# Preprocessing
X = pd.get_dummies(df[['Feature1', 'Feature2']])  # One-hot encoding for categorical variables
y = df['Class']

# Split the dataset into training and testing sets
X_train, X_test, y_train, y_test = train_test_split(X, y, test_size=0.2, random_state=42)

# Create a Decision Tree classifier
clf = DecisionTreeClassifier(random_state=42)

# Train the model
clf.fit(X_train, y_train)

# Make predictions
predictions = clf.predict(X_test)
```

```python
# Display the tree structure
tree_rules = export_text(clf,
feature_names=list(X.columns))
print(tree_rules)

# Output the predictions
print("Predictions:", predictions)
```

Dimensionality Reduction

Dimensionality reduction is a technique used in machine learning and statistics to reduce the number of input variables in a dataset while preserving as much information as possible. This is particularly useful when dealing with high-dimensional data, as it can help improve model performance, reduce computational cost, and mitigate the curse of dimensionality.

```python
from sklearn.decomposition import PCA
from sklearn.preprocessing import StandardScaler
import pandas as pd

# Sample dataset
df = pd.DataFrame({
    'Feature1': [2.5, 3.5, 1.5, 4.5],
    'Feature2': [2.5, 0.5, 2.0, 1.0],
    'Feature3': [1.0, 2.0, 3.0, 4.0]
})

# Standardizing the data
scaler = StandardScaler()
scaled_data = scaler.fit_transform(df)

# Applying PCA
pca = PCA(n_components=2)
reduced_data = pca.fit_transform(scaled_data)

print("Reduced Data:\n", reduced_data)
```

Frequent Pattern Growth

Frequent Pattern Growth (FP-Growth) is an efficient and scalable algorithm for mining frequent patterns, itemsets, and associations from large datasets. It is particularly useful in market basket analysis, where the goal is to find combinations of items that frequently co-occur in transactions.

```python
from mlxtend.frequent_patterns import fpgrowth
import pandas as pd

# Sample transaction data
transactions = [
    ['A', 'B', 'D'],
    ['B', 'C'],
    ['A', 'B', 'C', 'E'],
    ['B', 'E'],
    ['A', 'B', 'C', 'D']
]

# Create a DataFrame for transactions
df = pd.DataFrame({'transaction': transactions})

# One-hot encoding
onehot = df['transaction'].str.join('|').str.get_dummies()

# Apply FP-Growth algorithm
frequent_itemsets = fpgrowth(onehot, min_support=0.6, use_colnames=True)

print(frequent_itemsets)
```

K Means Clust

K-Means Clustering is an unsupervised machine learning algorithm used for partitioning a dataset into distinct clusters based on feature similarities. It aims to group data points into kkk clusters, where each data point belongs to the cluster with the nearest mean.

```python
import numpy as np
import matplotlib.pyplot as plt
from sklearn.cluster import KMeans

# Sample data points
X = np.array([[1, 2], [1, 4], [1, 0],
              [4, 2], [4, 4], [4, 0]])

# Define the number of clusters
k = 2

# Create KMeans model
kmeans = KMeans(n_clusters=k, random_state=0)

# Fit the model to the data
kmeans.fit(X)

# Get cluster labels and centroids
labels = kmeans.labels_
centroids = kmeans.cluster_centers_

# Print results
print("Cluster Labels:", labels)
print("Centroids:", centroids)

# Plotting
plt.scatter(X[:, 0], X[:, 1], c=labels, cmap='rainbow')
plt.scatter(centroids[:, 0], centroids[:, 1],
color='black', marker='x')  # Plot centroids
plt.title('K-Means Clustering')
plt.xlabel('X-axis')
plt.ylabel('Y-axis')
```

```
plt.show()
```

Linear Regression

Linear regression is a statistical method used to model the relationship between a dependent variable and one or more independent variables by fitting a linear equation to observed data. The goal is to predict the dependent variable (often called the target or output) based on the values of the independent variables (also called features or inputs).

```python
import numpy as np
import matplotlib.pyplot as plt
from sklearn.model_selection import train_test_split
from sklearn.linear_model import LinearRegression
from sklearn.metrics import mean_squared_error, r2_score

# Sample data
X = np.array([[1500], [1800], [2400], [3000], [3500]])
Y = np.array([300000, 400000, 500000, 600000, 700000])

# Split the data into training and testing sets
X_train, X_test, Y_train, Y_test = train_test_split(X, Y, test_size=0.2, random_state=0)

# Create a linear regression model
model = LinearRegression()

# Fit the model to the training data
model.fit(X_train, Y_train)

# Make predictions on the testing set
Y_pred = model.predict(X_test)

# Evaluate the model
mse = mean_squared_error(Y_test, Y_pred)
r2 = r2_score(Y_test, Y_pred)

# Print results
print("Mean Squared Error:", mse)
print("R-squared:", r2)
```

```python
# Plotting
plt.scatter(X, Y, color='blue', label='Actual Data')
plt.plot(X, model.predict(X), color='red', label='Fitted Line')
plt.title('Linear Regression')
plt.xlabel('Size (sq ft)')
plt.ylabel('Price ($)')
plt.legend()
plt.show()
```

Local Wighted Learning

Local Weighted Learning (LWL) is a type of machine learning technique that focuses on fitting a model locally, emphasizing data points that are closer to the target point being predicted. Unlike traditional models that consider the entire dataset equally, LWL assigns weights to data points based on their distance from the query point, allowing the model to adapt better to local patterns and variations in the data.

```python
import numpy as np
import matplotlib.pyplot as plt

class LocalWeightedLinearRegression:
    def __init__(self, tau=1.0):
        self.tau = tau  # Bandwidth parameter

    def _weights(self, X, xq):
        return np.exp(-np.sum((X - xq) ** 2, axis=1) / (2 * self.tau ** 2))

    def fit(self, X, y):
        self.X_train = X
        self.y_train = y

    def predict(self, Xq):
        predictions = []
        for xq in Xq:
            weights = self._weights(self.X_train, xq)
            weighted_X = self.X_train * weights[:, np.newaxis]
            weighted_y = self.y_train * weights

            # Fit a linear model using weighted least squares
            beta = np.linalg.inv(weighted_X.T @ weighted_X) @ (weighted_X.T @ weighted_y)
            predictions.append(beta[0] * xq + beta[1])  # y = beta[0]*x + beta[1]
        return np.array(predictions)
```

```python
# Sample data
X = np.array([[1], [2], [3], [4], [5], [6], [7], [8], [9], [10]])
y = np.array([1.5, 1.8, 2.5, 3.5, 5.0, 6.0, 6.5, 8.0, 8.5, 10.0])

# Fit the model
lwr = LocalWeightedLinearRegression(tau=1.5)
lwr.fit(X, y)

# Query points
Xq = np.linspace(1, 10, 100).reshape(-1, 1)
predictions = lwr.predict(Xq)

# Plotting
plt.scatter(X, y, color='blue', label='Training Data')
plt.plot(Xq, predictions, color='red', label='Local Weighted Linear Regression')
plt.title('Local Weighted Learning')
plt.xlabel('X')
plt.ylabel('Y')
plt.legend()
plt.show()
```

Logistic Regression

Logistic regression is a statistical method used for binary classification that predicts the probability of a binary outcome based on one or more predictor variables. Unlike linear regression, which predicts continuous outcomes, logistic regression predicts the probability that a given input point belongs to a certain class.

```python
import numpy as np
import matplotlib.pyplot as plt
from sklearn.model_selection import train_test_split
from sklearn.linear_model import LogisticRegression

# Sample data
X = np.array([[1], [2], [3], [4], [5], [6], [7], [8], [9], [10]])
y = np.array([0, 0, 0, 0, 1, 1, 1, 1, 1, 1])  # 0 = fail, 1 = pass

# Split the data into training and testing sets
X_train, X_test, y_train, y_test = train_test_split(X, y, test_size=0.2, random_state=42)

# Create a logistic regression model
model = LogisticRegression()

# Fit the model
model.fit(X_train, y_train)

# Make predictions
predictions = model.predict(X_test)
predicted_probabilities = model.predict_proba(X_test)[:, 1]  # Probability of class 1

# Plotting the decision boundary
plt.scatter(X, y, color='blue', label='Data Points')
x_boundary = np.linspace(0, 11, 100)
y_boundary = model.predict_proba(x_boundary.reshape(-1, 1))[:, 1]
```

```python
plt.plot(x_boundary, y_boundary, color='red',
label='Decision Boundary')
plt.title('Logistic Regression')
plt.xlabel('Study Hours')
plt.ylabel('Probability of Passing')
plt.legend()
plt.show()

# Print predictions
for i in range(len(X_test)):
    print(f'Study Hours: {X_test[i][0]}, Predicted Pass: {predictions[i]}, Probability: {predicted_probabilities[i]:.2f}')
```

Loss Functions

Loss functions, also known as cost functions or objective functions, measure the difference between the predicted values and the actual values in a model. They are crucial for training machine learning algorithms as they guide the optimization process. The goal of training is to minimize the loss function.

```python
import numpy as np

# Sample actual and predicted values for regression
y_true_regression = np.array([3, -0.5, 2, 7])
y_pred_regression = np.array([2.5, 0.0, 2, 8])

# Mean Squared Error
mse = np.mean((y_true_regression - y_pred_regression) ** 2)
print(f'Mean Squared Error: {mse}')

# Sample actual and predicted values for binary classification
y_true_classification = np.array([1, 0, 1, 1])
y_pred_classification = np.array([0.9, 0.1, 0.8, 0.6])

# Binary Cross-Entropy Loss
bce = -np.mean(y_true_classification * np.log(y_pred_classification) +
               (1 - y_true_classification) * np.log(1 - y_pred_classification))
print(f'Binary Cross-Entropy Loss: {bce}')
```

Lstm Prediction

Long Short-Term Memory (LSTM) networks are a type of recurrent neural network (RNN) particularly suited for sequence prediction tasks. They are designed to learn long-term dependencies, which makes them effective for time series forecasting, natural language processing, and other sequence-related tasks.

```python
import numpy as np
import pandas as pd
import matplotlib.pyplot as plt

# Generate synthetic time series data
def generate_time_series(seq_length):
    return np.sin(np.linspace(0, 100, seq_length)) + np.random.normal(scale=0.1, size=seq_length)

# Create dataset
data = generate_time_series(1000)
df = pd.DataFrame(data, columns=["Value"])
df.plot(title="Synthetic Time Series Data")
plt.show()
```

Neural Network

A Neural Network is a computational model inspired by the way biological neural networks in the human brain process information. It consists of interconnected groups of nodes, known as neurons, which work together to solve specific problems. Neural networks are particularly effective in recognizing patterns, making predictions, and classifying data. They are widely used in various applications, including image recognition, natural language processing, and game playing.

Activation Functions

Activation functions are mathematical functions used in neural networks to introduce non-linearity into the model. They determine the output of a neuron based on its input, allowing the network to learn complex patterns in the data. Without activation functions, the neural network would behave like a linear regression model, limiting its ability to solve more complex problems.

Binary Step

The Binary Step function is a simple activation function that outputs one of two values based on the input. It is a type of threshold activation function where the output is typically binary, making it useful in scenarios like binary classification tasks. However, its simplicity limits its effectiveness in more complex neural networks.

```python
import numpy as np

def binary_step(x):
    return np.where(x >= 0, 1, 0)  # Binary Step function

# Example Usage
input_data = np.array([-2, -1, 0, 1, 2])
output_data = binary_step(input_data)

print("Input Data:", input_data)    # Input Data: [-2 -1 0 1 2]
print("Binary Step Output:", output_data)
# Binary Step Output: [0 0 1 1 1]
```

Exponential Linear Unit

The Exponential Linear Unit (ELU) is an activation function designed to address the issues of traditional ReLU functions, such as the "dying ReLU" problem. The ELU function allows for negative outputs, which can help the network learn more effectively by providing non-zero gradients for negative input values.

```python
import numpy as np

def elu(x, alpha=1.0):
    return np.where(x > 0, x, alpha * (np.exp(x) - 1))  # ELU function

# Example Usage
input_data = np.array([-2, -1, 0, 1, 2])
output_data = elu(input_data)

print("Input Data:", input_data)
# Input Data: [-2 -1  0  1  2]
print("ELU Output:", output_data)
# ELU Output: [-0.86466472 -
0.63212056  0.          1.          2.         ]
```

Gaussian Error Unit

The Gaussian Error Unit (GEU) is an activation function inspired by the properties of the Gaussian distribution. It introduces non-linearity into the neural network while allowing for a differentiable output, which can improve the learning process and enhance model performance. GEU is particularly effective in cases where capturing variance is crucial.

```python
import numpy as np

def geu(x):
    return np.where(x >= 0, (1 / np.sqrt(2 * np.pi)) * np.exp(-0.5 * x**2), 0)  # GEU function

# Example Usage
input_data = np.array([-2, -1, 0, 1, 2])
output_data = geu(input_data)

print("Input Data:", input_data)
# Input Data: [-2 -1  0  1  2]
print("GEU Output:", output_data)
# GEU Output: [0.         0.24197072 0.39894228 0.24197072 0.05399097]
```

Leaky Rectified Linear unit

The Leaky Rectified Linear Unit (Leaky ReLU) is an activation function that aims to address the issue of "dying ReLU," where neurons can become inactive and stop learning during training. Unlike the standard ReLU function, which outputs zero for negative inputs, Leaky ReLU allows a small, non-zero, constant gradient (slope) for negative input values. This modification helps keep the neuron active and improves learning performance.

```python
import numpy as np

def leaky_relu(x, alpha=0.01):
    return np.where(x >= 0, x, alpha * x)  # Leaky ReLU function

# Example Usage
input_data = np.array([-2, -1, 0, 1, 2])
output_data = leaky_relu(input_data)

print("Input Data:", input_data)
# Input Data: [-2 -1  0  1  2]
print("Leaky ReLU Output:", output_data)
# Leaky ReLU Output: [-0.02 -0.01  0.    1.    2.  ]
```

mish

The Mish activation function is a non-monotonic activation function that aims to improve neural network performance by providing a smoother gradient compared to traditional activation functions like ReLU and its variants. Mish has shown promising results in various deep learning tasks, often yielding better performance in terms of convergence and generalization.

```python
import numpy as np

def mish(x):
    softplus = np.log1p(np.exp(x))   # Softplus function
    return x * np.tanh(softplus)     # Mish activation

# Example Usage
input_data = np.array([-2, -1, 0, 1, 2])
output_data = mish(input_data)

print("Input Data:", input_data)
# Input Data: [-2 -1  0  1  2]
print("Mish Output:", output_data)
# Mish Output: [-0.8659 -0.3160  0.      0.7616  1.7175]
```

squareplus

The Squareplus activation function is defined mathematically as $f(x)=x^2+xf(x) = x^2 + xf(x)=x^2+x$. It combines the properties of a quadratic function and a linear function, allowing for a smooth transition while enhancing the output for positive inputs. The function is particularly useful in neural networks as it introduces non-linearity and helps to model complex relationships.

```python
import numpy as np

def squareplus(x):
    return x**2 + x  # Squareplus calculation

# Example Usage
input_data = np.array([-2, -1, 0, 1, 2])
output_data = squareplus(input_data)

print("Input Data:", input_data)
# Input Data: [-2 -1  0  1  2]
print("Squareplus Output:", output_data)
# Squareplus Output: [ 0  0  0  2  6]
```

Convultion Neural Network

Convolutional Neural Networks (CNNs) are a class of deep learning models designed primarily for processing structured grid data, such as images. They leverage convolutional layers to automatically extract and learn spatial hierarchies of features from input data. CNNs have revolutionized the field of computer vision, enabling advances in image recognition, classification, and segmentation.

```python
import tensorflow as tf
from tensorflow.keras import layers, models

# Build the CNN model
def create_cnn_model(input_shape, num_classes):
    model = models.Sequential()
    # Convolutional Layer
    model.add(layers.Conv2D(32, (3, 3), activation='relu', input_shape=input_shape))
    model.add(layers.MaxPooling2D((2, 2)))

    model.add(layers.Conv2D(64, (3, 3), activation='relu'))
    model.add(layers.MaxPooling2D((2, 2)))

    model.add(layers.Conv2D(64, (3, 3), activation='relu'))

    # Flattening and Fully Connected Layers
    model.add(layers.Flatten())
    model.add(layers.Dense(64, activation='relu'))
    model.add(layers.Dense(num_classes, activation='softmax'))  # Output layer

    return model

# Example Usage
input_shape = (64, 64, 3)  # Example input shape (image height, width, channels)
num_classes = 10  # Example number of classes
cnn_model = create_cnn_model(input_shape, num_classes)

# Model Summary
```

```
cnn_model.summary()
```

Simple Neural Network

A Simple Neural Network consists of interconnected layers of nodes (neurons) designed to recognize patterns in data. The most basic form is a feedforward neural network, which consists of an input layer, one or more hidden layers, and an output layer. Each neuron in one layer connects to every neuron in the next layer, and each connection has an associated weight.

```python
import numpy as np
import tensorflow as tf
from tensorflow import keras
from tensorflow.keras import layers

# Generate synthetic data
X_train = np.random.rand(1000, 10)  # 1000 samples, 10 features
y_train = np.random.randint(2, size=(1000, 1))  # Binary labels (0 or 1)

# Build the Simple Neural Network model
def create_simple_nn(input_shape):
    model = keras.Sequential()
    model.add(layers.Dense(16, activation='relu', input_shape=input_shape))  # Hidden Layer
    model.add(layers.Dense(1, activation='sigmoid'))  # Output Layer

    return model

# Example Usage
input_shape = (10,)  # Number of features
simple_nn = create_simple_nn(input_shape)

# Compile the model
simple_nn.compile(optimizer='adam', loss='binary_crossentropy', metrics=['accuracy'])

# Train the model
simple_nn.fit(X_train, y_train, epochs=10, batch_size=32)
```

```python
# Evaluate the model
loss, accuracy = simple_nn.evaluate(X_train, y_train)
print(f'Loss: {loss}, Accuracy: {accuracy}')
```

Two Hidden Layers

A Simple Neural Network with Two Hidden Layers enhances the model's capacity to learn complex patterns in data. By adding another hidden layer, the network can learn more intricate representations and relationships in the input data. This structure is particularly useful in scenarios where the data has non-linear relationships that a single-layer network may not capture effectively.

```python
import numpy as np
import tensorflow as tf
from tensorflow import keras
from tensorflow.keras import layers

# Generate synthetic data
X_train = np.random.rand(1000, 10)  # 1000 samples, 10 features
y_train = np.random.randint(2, size=(1000, 1))  # Binary labels (0 or 1)

# Build the Simple Neural Network model with two hidden layers
def create_nn_with_two_hidden_layers(input_shape):
    model = keras.Sequential()
    model.add(layers.Dense(16, activation='relu', input_shape=input_shape))  # First Hidden Layer
    model.add(layers.Dense(8, activation='relu'))  # Second Hidden Layer
    model.add(layers.Dense(1, activation='sigmoid'))  # Output Layer

    return model

# Example Usage
input_shape = (10,)  # Number of features
nn_with_two_layers = create_nn_with_two_hidden_layers(input_shape)

# Compile the model
```

```python
nn_with_two_layers.compile(optimizer='adam', 
loss='binary_crossentropy', metrics=['accuracy'])

# Train the model
nn_with_two_layers.fit(X_train, y_train, epochs=10, 
batch_size=32)

# Evaluate the model
loss, accuracy = nn_with_two_layers.evaluate(X_train, 
y_train)
print(f'Loss: {loss}, Accuracy: {accuracy}')
```

Graphs

Graphs are abstract data structures that consist of nodes (also known as vertices) and edges, which represent connections between the nodes. Graphs are widely used in computer science and mathematics to model relationships between objects, such as networks, social connections, or paths between cities.

A Star

A* is a popular pathfinding and graph traversal algorithm, commonly used for finding the shortest path from a start node to a goal node in a weighted graph.

```python
import heapq

# Heuristic function: Manhattan distance
def heuristic(a, b):
    return abs(a[0] - b[0]) + abs(a[1] - b[1])

# A* Algorithm
def a_star(grid, start, goal):
    rows, cols = len(grid), len(grid[0])
    open_set = []
    heapq.heappush(open_set, (0, start))
    came_from = {}
    g_score = {start: 0}
    f_score = {start: heuristic(start, goal)}

    while open_set:
        _, current = heapq.heappop(open_set)

        if current == goal:
            # Reconstruct path
            path = []
            while current in came_from:
                path.append(current)
                current = came_from[current]
            return path[::-1]

        neighbors = [(0, 1), (1, 0), (0, -1), (-1, 0)]  # 4-way movement
        for dx, dy in neighbors:
            neighbor = (current[0] + dx, current[1] + dy)
            if 0 <= neighbor[0] < rows and 0 <= neighbor[1] < cols and grid[neighbor[0]][neighbor[1]] == 0:
                tentative_g_score = g_score[current] + 1
```

```python
                if tentative_g_score < g_score.get(neighbor, float('inf')):
                    came_from[neighbor] = current
                    g_score[neighbor] = tentative_g_score
                    f_score[neighbor] = tentative_g_score + heuristic(neighbor, goal)
                    heapq.heappush(open_set, (f_score[neighbor], neighbor))

    return None  # No path found

# Example usage
grid = [
    [0, 1, 0, 0, 0],
    [0, 1, 0, 1, 0],
    [0, 0, 0, 1, 0],
    [0, 1, 0, 0, 0],
    [0, 0, 0, 1, 0]
]
start = (0, 0)
goal = (4, 4)
path = a_star(grid, start, goal)

print("Path:", path)
```

Ant Colony Optimization

Ant Colony Optimization (ACO) is a bio-inspired algorithm modeled on the behavior of real ants searching for food. Ants deposit pheromones along their path, and over time, shorter paths accumulate more pheromones, guiding other ants toward those paths.

```python
import random

# Distance between cities (symmetric TSP example)
distances = [[0, 2, 9, 10],
             [1, 0, 6, 4],
             [15, 7, 0, 8],
             [6, 3, 12, 0]]

# ACO Parameters
num_ants = 5
num_iterations = 100
alpha = 1        # Pheromone importance
beta = 2         # Distance importance
evaporation_rate = 0.5
pheromone_constant = 100

# Initialize pheromones
num_cities = len(distances)
pheromones = [[1 for _ in range(num_cities)] for _ in range(num_cities)]

# Helper: Get tour length
def get_tour_length(tour):
    return sum(distances[tour[i]][tour[i + 1]] for i in range(len(tour) - 1)) + distances[tour[-1]][tour[0]]

# Helper: Select next city based on pheromone and distance
def select_next_city(pheromones, current_city, unvisited):
    probabilities = []
    for city in unvisited:
        prob = (pheromones[current_city][city] ** alpha) * ((1 / distances[current_city][city]) ** beta)
```

```python
        probabilities.append(prob)
    total_prob = sum(probabilities)
    probabilities = [prob / total_prob for prob in probabilities]
    return random.choices(unvisited, probabilities)[0]

# Ant Colony Optimization algorithm
def aco():
    best_tour = None
    best_length = float('inf')

    for _ in range(num_iterations):
        all_tours = []
        for _ in range(num_ants):
            tour = [random.randint(0, num_cities - 1)]
            unvisited = set(range(num_cities)) - {tour[0]}
            while unvisited:
                next_city = select_next_city(pheromones, tour[-1], list(unvisited))
                tour.append(next_city)
                unvisited.remove(next_city)
            all_tours.append(tour)

        # Update pheromones
        for i in range(num_cities):
            for j in range(num_cities):
                pheromones[i][j] *= (1 - evaporation_rate)

        for tour in all_tours:
            length = get_tour_length(tour)
            for i in range(len(tour) - 1):
                pheromones[tour[i]][tour[i + 1]] += pheromone_constant / length
            pheromones[tour[-1]][tour[0]] += pheromone_constant / length

            if length < best_length:
                best_tour, best_length = tour, length
```

```python
    return best_tour, best_length

# Example usage
best_tour, best_length = aco()
print("Best Tour:", best_tour)
print("Tour Length:", best_length)
```

Breadth First Search

Breadth-First Search (BFS) is an algorithm for traversing or searching through a graph or tree. It explores all the vertices at the present depth before moving on to vertices at the next depth level. BFS is often used to find the shortest path in unweighted graphs or to explore all nodes in a breadthwise manner.

```python
from collections import deque

def bfs(graph, start):
    visited = set()
    queue = deque([start])
    visited.add(start)

    while queue:
        node = queue.popleft()
        print(node, end=" ")

        for neighbor in graph[node]:
            if neighbor not in visited:
                queue.append(neighbor)
                visited.add(neighbor)

# Example Usage
graph = {
    'A': ['B', 'C'],
    'B': ['A', 'D', 'E'],
    'C': ['A', 'F'],
    'D': ['B'],
    'E': ['B', 'F'],
    'F': ['C', 'E']
}

bfs(graph, 'A')
```

Check Bipatrite

A graph is **bipartite** if its vertices can be divided into two disjoint sets such that no two vertices within the same set are adjacent. A graph is bipartite if it can be colored using two colors in such a way that no two adjacent vertices share the same color.

```python
from collections import deque

def is_bipartite(graph, start):
    color = {}
    queue = deque([start])
    color[start] = 0  # Assign the first color (0)

    while queue:
        node = queue.popleft()

        for neighbor in graph[node]:
            if neighbor not in color:
                # Assign the opposite color to the neighbor
                color[neighbor] = 1 - color[node]
                queue.append(neighbor)
            elif color[neighbor] == color[node]:
                return False  # Same color detected, not bipartite
    return True

# Example Usage
graph = {
    0: [1, 3],
    1: [0, 2],
    2: [1, 3],
    3: [0, 2]
}

print(is_bipartite(graph, 0))   # Output: True (Graph is bipartite)
```

Check Cycle

Detecting a cycle in a graph is a fundamental problem in graph theory. A cycle occurs when a path starts and ends at the same vertex with at least one edge traversed. We can use Depth-First Search (DFS) for directed and undirected graphs to check for cycles.

```python
def has_cycle(graph):
    visited = set()

    def dfs(node, parent):
        visited.add(node)
        for neighbor in graph[node]:
            if neighbor not in visited:
                if dfs(neighbor, node):
                    return True
            elif neighbor != parent:
                return True  # Cycle detected
        return False

    for v in graph:
        if v not in visited:
            if dfs(v, -1):  # Start DFS with no parent (-1)
                return True
    return False

# Example Usage
graph = {
    0: [1],
    1: [0, 2],
    2: [1, 3],
    3: [2, 4],
    4: [3, 1]  # This creates a cycle between 1, 2, 3, 4
}

print(has_cycle(graph))  # Output: True (Graph contains a cycle)
```

Connected Components

A connected component is a subset of vertices such that there is a path between any two vertices in this subset. A graph can have multiple connected components. This is particularly useful for analyzing the structure of a graph and understanding how nodes are related.

```python
def connected_components(graph):
    visited = set()
    components = []

    def dfs(node, component):
        visited.add(node)
        component.append(node)
        for neighbor in graph[node]:
            if neighbor not in visited:
                dfs(neighbor, component)

    for v in graph:
        if v not in visited:
            component = []
            dfs(v, component)
            components.append(component)

    return components

# Example Usage
graph = {
    0: [1],
    1: [0, 2],
    2: [1],
    3: [4],
    4: [3, 5],
    5: [4]
}

print(connected_components(graph))
# Output: [[0, 1, 2], [3, 4, 5]]
# Two connected components
```

Finding Fridges

The task is to find all the fridges from a given list of appliances based on specific criteria. This could involve searching through a list of items, identifying which ones are fridges based on their characteristics, and potentially filtering or counting them.

```python
class Appliance:
    def __init__(self, name, appliance_type):
        self.name = name
        self.type = appliance_type

def find_fridges(appliances):
    return [appliance.name for appliance in appliances if appliance.type == 'fridge']

# Example Usage
appliance_list = [
    Appliance("Whirlpool", "fridge"),
    Appliance("LG Washing Machine", "washing machine"),
    Appliance("Samsung Fridge", "fridge"),
    Appliance("Oven", "oven"),
    Appliance("GE Fridge", "fridge"),
]

fridges = find_fridges(appliance_list)
print(fridges)
# Output: ['Whirlpool', 'Samsung Fridge', 'GE Fridge']
```

In every line of code, they have woven a story of innovation and creativity. This book has been your compass in the vast world of Python.

Close this chapter knowing that every challenge overcome is an achievement, and every solution is a step toward mastery.

Your code is the melody that gives life to projects. May they continue creating and programming with passion!

Thank you for allowing me to be part of your journey.

With gratitude,

Hernando Abella

Author of 300+ Python Algorithms

Discover Other Useful Resources at:
www.beat-byte-publishing.com/

Get your Bonus Books at:
www.hernandoabella.com

ALUNA PUBLISHING HOUSE

Thank you for trusting our Publishing House. If you could evaluate our work and give us a review on Amazon, we will appreciate it very much!
Scan this code to leave an honest review:

Or go to: **https://www.amazon.com/review/create-review/?ie=UTF8&channel=glance-detail&asin=B0DJH27Q19**
Thanks (again!)

This Book may not be copied or printed without the permission of the author.
COPYRIGHT 2024 ALUNA PUBLISHING HOUSE
ISBN : 979-8341171770